# HEARST MARINE BOOKS
# KAYAK CAMPING

# HEARST MARINE BOOKS
# KAYAK CAMPING

## David Harrison

### Illustrations by Ron Carboni

**HEARST MARINE BOOKS**
New York

It is the policy of William Morrow and Company, Inc., and its imprints and affiliates, recognizing the importance of preserving what has been written, to print the books we publish on acid-free paper, and we exert our best efforts to that end.

Library of Congress Cataloguing-in-Publication Data

Harrison, David, 1938-
    Hearst Marine Books kayak camping / David Harrison;
    illustrations by Ron Carboni.
        p.          cm.
    Includes index.
    ISBN 0-688-13249-9
    1. Kayaking—United States. 2. Camping—United States.
    I. Title.      II. Title: Kayak camping.
GV790.H37      1995
797.1'224'0973—dc20                                        94-39488
                                                               CIP

Printed in the United States of America

First Edition

1 2 3 4 5 6 7 8 9 10

Produced for Hearst Books by
Michael Mouland & Associates,
Toronto

Book design by Mimi Maxwell

# ACKNOWLEDGMENTS

No one is born with a genetic predisposition for sleeping on the ground. We learn camping skills from a parent, a camp counselor, or friends. I had all of these benefits, and was fortunate, as well, to marry a woman who shared my love of the outdoors. Judy has put in thousands of miles of paddling with me. She has faced river rapids and storm-tossed seas, toiled across the portage trails and, in the face of utter exhaustion, not infrequently in a downpour, prepared creative and nourishing meals for a famished crew. Then she earned the reward of sleeping on the ground.

This book is based on over thirty years of canoe and kayak camping experience, and throughout the book I have used the plural *we*. Such references are likely to be a composite of skills, observations, techniques, and camping philosophies shared—often learned through trial and error—with Judy. Her special interest is the kitchen, but her training and skills as a CPR instructor and certified EMT (emergency medical technician) made it possible for us and many of our adventurous friends to march off into the wilderness with greater confidence, knowing there was a person with both practical and learned first-aid skills among us.

In reality, the authorship of this book is shared with my wife, since the experiences that give rise to its contents would simply not have been possible without her partnership.

Special thanks are also due to Lee and Judy Moyer, proprietors of Pacific Water Sports in Seattle. The Moyers are true pioneers in the sport and pastime known as "sea kayaking," which, until recently, had only a cult following. They helped introduce Judy and me to the sport and to the coastal environment so that we could be as comfortable there as we had been for many years canoeing the inland seas and rivers.

# CONTENTS

# INTRODUCTION

Camping conjures up anything from pitching a tent in the backyard to spending a month in an RV park. It may also sound like backpacking, which was just coming into vogue when I was in college, as a sort of adjunct to the hippie life. Backpackers—or "bark eaters," as they were sometimes called—had a decidedly downscale, unwashed image. Since I was headed straight into the business world as a Wall Street banker—a "suit," we might say today—backpacking didn't quite fit my self-image.

Fortunately, my introduction to camping was by way of a canoe, so I never had to live like a mole in a backpacker's tent, and avoided, as well, the opprobrium attached to such a lowbrow pursuit. Whether, in fact, canoe camping is higher in the evolutionary order than backpacking is debatable, but at the time I perceived it to be a more blessed calling and pursued it with a zealot's passion. Later in life, I was introduced to kayaking—the whitewater kind. Whitewater kayakers are mostly car campers; that is, they may head into the mountains with almost the same equipage as the RVers. Without big lanterns, double-burner Coleman stoves, inflatable air mats for the back of the van or giant umbrella tents, we were out-of-car-doorsmen for whom camping was either an economic necessity or, in the case of our more remote venues on Planet Dirt, the only way to get a night's sleep within a hundred miles.

For the truly driven whitewater kayaker, multi-day self-support trips on the longer western rivers became the goal. The idea was to avoid the necessity of raft support, or in some cases to bootleg a trip on a permit river, swooping in and out before the uniforms could nab you. Some rivers were too difficult—especially those with mandatory portages—for the rafts; the only practical solution was self-support. Cramming enough food and gear into a whitewater boat for even an overnight trip would be a challenge for the most avid bark eater.

Self-support river running is an intricate puzzle, and I've included a chapter on the topic. Even if you never plan to take a self-supported river kayak trip, it's worth reading. You'll gain an appreciation of what backpackers face, and you'll see just how little it really takes to be warm, dry, and well fed in the roughest of outdoor settings. And, as you'll discover in the chapter on boats, there are a few skinny little British-style sea kayaks out there that are almost as space-constrained as a whitewater boat.

This book assumes that you have learned basic paddling and navigation skills in a touring or sea kayak and are comfortable in your ability to get on and off the water. You are able to cover five to ten, or more, miles in a day's paddling. In an earlier book, *Sea Kayaking Basics*, I included only one short chapter on camping, placed at the end of the book to suggest that, in fact, the real reason for learning to kayak was to go camping. As with any outdoor activity, the closer to home, and to the road, the more likely it is that you will be sharing your experience with a crowd. That crowd may be more interested in the size of their boom box or whether the beer is going to hold out than in enjoying nature on its own terms. So the object is to put a little distance between you and the parking lot—and the more distance, the more likely you are to enjoy the beauty and serenity that the out-of-doors represents. Even if there's a small crowd, at least you will be in the company of folks who share your goal of quiet enjoyment.

The kayak, like the canoe, is a veritable magic carpet to a wonderful outdoor world. The ocean environment is especially alluring with its incredible diversity of life above, below, and on the water. No craft is so uniquely suited to the exploration of islands, and coastlines, worldwide. Places that the yachtsman can see only through his binoculars are accessible to the kayaker. Having the requisite paddling and navigation skills is mandatory, but having the outdoor survival and camping skills opens up a huge vista of water travel and exploration by kayak.

It is ironic that in general, the closer you are to civilization the harder it is to find a suitable camp. I don't get into urban camping in this book, but am reminded of a wonderful story published in *Canoe* magazine some years back by two guys who circumnavigated Manhattan Island in a canoe and set up camp on an old railroad bridge abutment in the middle of the Hudson River.

## KNOW YOUR LIMITS

I do emphasize the desirability of possessing a certain level of kayak-paddling proficiency and do suggest that you feel comfortable with chart and compass and finding your way. Understanding the tides and being familiar with launching and landing in at least small surf would also be desirable. Knowing your paddling speed and level of endurance—how many miles you can expect to paddle in a day—is important because campsites in the open-water kayaker's environment are not always around the corner—or the next one! In some coastal environments, even ones that are entirely public, the places where you can set up a camp may be few and far between. I've seen "campsites" that were two acres of white sand at low tide shrink to a ten-by-twelve shelf at high tide. The ability to make the mileage and identify the one bay in fifty that hides a suitable campsite may make the difference between having a great adventure or a time of fretful anxiety—or worse.

But acquiring those skills is worth the effort. The kayak as a camping vehicle is unexcelled. There is much more capacity, and therefore comfort, than any backpacker ever dreamed of, and the explosion of interest in kayak touring comes at a time when there has never been such an array of equipment choices. Maybe that's more than coincidence. Some of these items are toys, of course, but many more of the available equipment choices are, in fact, the product of new technologies that have made possible creature comforts we never dreamed of twenty years ago. Some of us would be loath to admit that we've lost our appetite for the deprivations we willingly—even enthusiastically—suffered in the good old days, but certainly recent advances in outdoor technology have made camping an even more enjoyable lifelong pursuit.

Before we go any further, let me make my own philosophy of camping known. I don't believe that one's prowess as a camper is measured by the amount of misery or deprivation endured (the British explorers and their apostles have this predilection); rather, success is measured by one's ability to travel, eat, sleep, play, and enjoy, all the while maintaining both a safe and pleasant hygiene, no matter how long the trip or rugged the environment. One should be able to emerge from a week-long trip or a month's expedition well fed, well rested, clean-shaven (though that's purely a matter of personal choice!), and certainly in superior physical condition compared with one's friends who spent their vacation at a $200-a-day golf or tennis resort.

Kayak camping is a physical, mental, and experiential activity. Even a short, simple itinerary will enhance your physical well-being. An extended trip can put you in the kind of physical condition even a triathlete could respect. As we get into the area of trip planning and execution in this book, you will come to appreciate the planning, or mental, component of this game. Few sensations compare to the experience it-self: the feeling of flying on water, of being intimately connected to your environment; enjoying the infinite scenic possibilities, fauna and flora, perhaps even finding yourself surrounded by a colony of seals or a pod of whales—there simply are more stimuli for your senses than can be found in any other natural environment. Yes, I am going to describe a vast array of boats and equipment, and you can spend a bundle if you're so inclined, but at its most basic level (and perhaps its best), this activity is affordable, even cheap.

Kayak camping can be a solitary pursuit, a social event, or an adventure with a small group of expeditioners. It can and should be a family activity. Kids can be included at almost any age, the younger the better. I've experienced all of these modes, and there never has been and never will be enough time to actualize all of the dreams I've dreamed or even the plans I've made.

# HEARST MARINE BOOKS
# KAYAK CAMPING

# A BACKPACK ON THE WATER

Two of us were camped on a moderately busy island in the San Juans, a popular boating area north of Seattle. These are developed campsites, almost suburban in nature, that attract not only sea kayakers but powerboaters and sailors, the latter usually stir crazy after more than twenty-four hours cooped up in their little galleons. Normally, the sailors will use their dinghies to ferry themselves and gear from boat to campsite to enjoy for a short while what kayak campers take for granted.

Two such sailors were camped next to us, and as we prepared to pack up our kayaks and take off for the next island to the north, they watched, astounded at the pile of gear growing at the water's edge. They were no strangers to the transport of camping equipment by small boat, and they bantered with us about the likelihood of cramming this small mountain of equipage into our skinny little boats. "You'll never do it," pronounced the elder sailor. And that, in fact, is the reaction of virtually any bystander on the docks, shorelines, and boat ramps from which I have embarked over the years. He would shortly be proven wrong, of course.

The marketing manager for one of the kayak manufacturers was exhibiting boats at a large outdoor show in Chicago when a curious showgoer stopped to examine the boats on display in the booth. Noting the small circumference of the hatches, this person asked, "How do you get your backpack into these?" The manufacturer said simply, "This kayak is the backpack."

## HOW BIG IS A BACKPACK?

The kayak manufacturer might well have said, "This boat is four backpacks." I own a pack that may be the Mother of All Backpacks—for winter camping and all the bulk that activity requires—with close to five thousand cubic inches of capacity. Large backpacks usually advertise a load capacity of between three thousand and four thousand cubic inches. Those figures are interior space, so you might add another three hun-

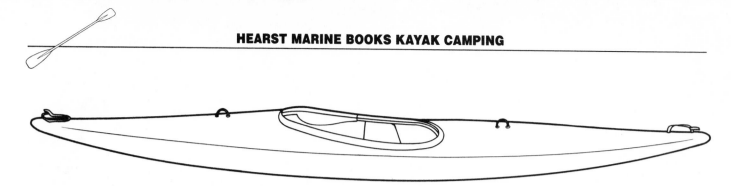

**Whitewater kayak**

dred to five hundred additional cubes for some of those items that can be appended to or dangled from the pack. Kayak manufacturers don't advertise their boats by cubic inches of capacity, but designate them as being of small, medium, or large capacity (I have seen some gallonage figures, but this doesn't relate well to usable storage capacity). By my own calculations, a medium-sized touring kayak offers storage capacity of eighteen thousand to twenty thousand cubic inches. That doesn't include the pieces of gear that may be strapped to the deck or carried in your lap.

The point is that even a small kayak represents a huge premium in carrying capacity when compared with even the most commodious backpack. Not to mention that schlepping a five-thousand-cubic-inch, fully-loaded pack more than five hundred yards could prove dangerous to your health. If the concept of cubic inches seems remote, consider weight. Most backpackers will try to keep their load under sixty pounds, regardless of their pack's theoretical capacity. What's important is being able to man-haul the load from point A to point B. Consider the hauling capacity of a sea kayak: Including the gallonage (as much as five gallons per single kayak) of fresh water that must be carried by  a sea kayaker headed into British Columbia's Barkley Sound, for example, it would not be unusual for a single sea kayak to be weighed down by 150 pounds of food, water, and gear for a week's trip.

## THE GEAR HOG VS. THE MINIMALIST

The amount of carrying capacity is not the sole criterion for choosing a boat, as we will see in a later chapter, but doing a self-evaluation will help determine your boat selection. Actually, the size of your boat may be only incidentally related to your appetite for carrying space—or lack of it. Many people will choose a large boat because they are large people, or a large boat may be the stable boat they desire for other reasons. There is a tendency among people of any size to fill any pack, be it on their bike or their back, to its absolute capacity, even if they don't need a down-filled parka for their day trip in the temperate zone. And, certainly, there is no need to fill every cubic inch of your 18½-foot kayak just because it's there.

Which brings us to the real crux of the matter. Are you one who revels in your equipment and feels compelled to bring not only every conceivable creature comfort but a change of clothes for every day out—or more if you must "get dressed up" for dinner—and do you look upon camping as an excuse to eat like a gourmand? That's a fair description of the trips my wife and I plan with our friends. Or are you a Natty Bumppo wannabe, who can sleep curled up in a hollow log, change only your socks on a two-week trip, and supplement your granola with nuts and berries gathered en route?

I don't know too many of my paddling friends who go to the latter extreme—their breed apparently died off some time ago—but I do, in fact, take solo trips and some aggressive small-group (no more than four persons) commando trips where packing light is both necessary and desirable. Consider, for example, an itinerary that calls for covering fifteen, twenty, or more miles a day and that you will travel, making and breaking camp, every day. Such a trip plan will dictate less gear, lighter gear, and foodstuffs that can be prepared quickly and easily. As we will see later, the amount of time spent making and breaking camp is a major factor in trip planning.

So which are you? Well, like me, you may end up being both. The good news is that if you are a gear hog by inclination and choice, you can rest easy. There are few creature comforts that can't be satisfied by today's vast selection of camping equipment, and there may still be room left over for toys that have nothing to do with comfort. Forget the boom box, but I know that on a recent two-week kayak trip our outfit contained at least ten pounds of books—fiction, nonfiction, bird-watching manuals, edible-plant books, you name it. Everyone had his or her own camera, and spread among the group of us were several pairs of binoculars, a crab trap, an espresso maker—you get the picture.

## BOAT COMPARISON

The whitewater kayaker who chooses to do a self-support river trip is as constrained as the backpacker; he or she is a minimalist by necessity. Some whitewater boats have considerably more volume than others, but even the largest will force a frugal selection of gear, and granola may, in fact, constitute a fair portion of your calories (self-support river running is specifically covered in Chapter 10). The next largest classification of boats is river-touring kayaks, which attempt to preserve some of the maneuverability of a whitewater boat, but are longer and more straight-keeled and possess considerably more volume. They might compare to my winter-camping backpack. Sea kayaks range from skinny British-style boats to giant expedition boats. The former are barely more capacious than a big whitewater boat; the latter will allow you to bring your teddy bear and guitar.

Finally, there are double sea kayaks. These also come in a range of sizes from stingy to opulent. A small double is a tight situation for even the minimalist when you realize that most of the stern paddler's legs fill up the midsection of the boat, and compared with two single kayaks, the equivalent of one stern section (or bow section, if you prefer) is missing. The largest double sea kayaks, however, rival the largest expedition canoes. Here's another thought if you are a family, or a couple, considering the merits of a double

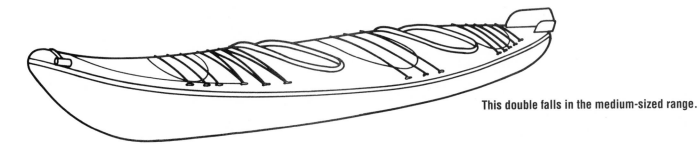

This double falls in the medium-sized range.

3

kayak versus one or more singles: Yes, two medium-volume singles will carry more gear than a medium-sized double, but the width and depth of a double kayak are normally greater than that of a single kayak, which means you can accommodate packs or individual pieces of gear in a double that just won't fit into a single. For example, we have a wooden kitchen box that fits nicely in the midsection of our double; I don't know of any single kayak that could accommodate it. Want to take a two-burner Coleman stove? That might just be a reason to choose one kayak over another, single or double.

## BOAT PERFORMANCE

When we get into the subject of specific boat designs and their suitability for various styles of camping, we'll be considering a lot of dimensions: length, width, depth, and various hull shapes. The performance characteristics of virtually any kayak will be altered by the introduction of a heavy load. Only a few kayaks are actually designed to achieve optimal performance when fully loaded. Most will experience a degradation in performance; they will turn slower, wallow, yaw, or just plain go slower. As we will learn in the section on packing a boat, the distribution of a load can have major effect. For the moment, you may want to remember the point made earlier that you don't need to fill every cubic inch of space just because it's there. We may be at an advantage over the backpacker who gets no free glide, but at some point the weight and number of pieces in our load have a cost attached. If you are going to pack and push a big load, is the effort more than compensated for by the level of comfort you expect to enjoy when you do get your load to camp?

4

# 2

# WHERE TO GO KAYAK CAMPING

## COMMERCIAL OUTFITTERS

If you are a newcomer to camping of any kind, or just new to camping out of a kayak, your best bet is to go on a trip with someone who is experienced. Kayak camping may not be as high up the ladder of camping complexity as snow camping in winter, but it presents enough challenges to make apprenticeship a wise option. A good choice is a commercial or "packaged" trip, where you may only be required to show up with your own toothbrush. The outfitter will take care of virtually every other detail of food, equipment, and the itinerary. All you have to do is follow the leader's directions, ask plenty of questions, and take note of what and why. Most of these trips are participatory; in other words, you are expected to take part in the work. You have to carry your weight with a paddle, of course, but you'll be loading and unloading the kayaks, making and breaking camp, helping with kitchen chores, setting up the privy, or whatever.

Commercial trips are recommended especially if you have not yet made major purchases of paddling or camping equipment. A careful study of the outfitter's selections and inquiries into why he or she chose such equipment will give you a good data base when you go shopping for your own gear. There are, to be sure, outfitters who skimp, but the best ones have generally chosen gear that is tough and reliable, representing a major investment for that outfitter. Since your main objective is to figure out how to plan and execute your own trips, make sure the outfitter spends some time going over the itinerary and charts with you. Why has he or she chosen this particular area? What permits, restrictions, special features, or hazards will you encounter? What sort of paddling distances will you be expected to cover, and what are the safety valves if the weather deteriorates? Are open fires permitted? What are the arrangements for camp hygiene (water availability, human waste disposal, etc.)? Will you be camping on rock, sand, grass, or none of the above? How will wind and tides affect your plan?

The risk in a commercially outfitted trip is that you might be simply expected to follow the leader like sheep. Try to avoid such a program, or be a pest about getting the leader to go over the charts with you, keeping you and others in your group posted as to where you are, where you are headed, and why. You are there to learn, not to be treated to a Disneyland travelogue.

## CLUBS

Taking a trip with experienced friends or with a club group is another option. If you are going to put yourself in the hands of friends or acquaintances, you'll have to be your own judge of the quality of leadership, judgment, and potential for learning the ropes. In the case of club trips, the club's own history will have to be your guide. I am familiar with a dozen or more clubs around the country, which is hardly the basis for a comprehensive evaluation. But these clubs take themselves and their programs seriously. Most trip leaders have met club-imposed criteria, and the trips they lead have been graded by degree of difficulty. By way of example I have extracted the chart on page 7 to illustrate how one club classifies its sea kayaking trips. There are as many rating systems as there are clubs, but spending a few minutes studying this example can serve as a self-evaluation. In other words, would you feel comfortable on an SK III trip?

Each winter, this particular club publishes a new schedule of trips for the coming year. A brief description of the trip, the date, and the leader's name and phone number are the common elements. You can usually obtain club names for your area from a local retailer of paddle-sports equipment. See also the Appendix in this book. A club may or may not have *canoe* or *kayak* in the name. Two large and venerable clubs come to mind: the Appalachian Mountain Club in the northeast and the Mountaineers in the Pacific Northwest; both offer full schedules of sea kayaking trips.

## ORGANIZED AREAS VS. WILDERNESS

*Wilderness* is a word that has lost some of its cachet. First of all, there is very little of what could truly be called wilderness left on the planet. Even if the road doesn't go there, someone has surely scanned and cataloged it for some manner of resource plunder. Today's wilderness is tomorrow's condo development or mining venture. Even the old-fashioned concept of wilderness is a bit suspect, since it was the advancing army of European settlers, "more numerous than the leaves on the trees," who characterized the land as a wilderness. This implied an inhospitable environment, but the land had of course sustained several thousand years of habitation and cultural development by the native peoples, whose domain was shortly to be appropriated and "improved" by the new arrivals.

This is not a political tract, so we will continue to use the term *wilderness* to refer to those areas that are remote, undeveloped, largely uninhabited, and accessible only with difficulty or ingenuity. In a true wilderness you should expect to see few recent signs of man, no trail markers, and the available information might be no more than a general description (no guidebooks). What we usually find are patches of wilderness, which if we walk for half a day, mountain-bike for three hours, or paddle for a day, we will come to the bridge, the county road, the pipeline, or the guest ranch.

Nevertheless, the illusion is a nice one. Most of us spend our outdoor time searching out and celebrating those remaining patches of wilderness. It is also no surprise that the tremendous

## SEA KAYAK TRIP CLASSIFICATION

| Trip Rating | SK I | SK II | SK III | SK IV | SK V | SK VI |
|---|---|---|---|---|---|---|
| **Geography** (*Fetch* is defined as the unobstructed distance which the wind can blow over the water and build up waves.) nm. = nautical mile | In areas protected from waves by nearby landforms in case of wind | Fetches less than 10 nm. unless it is generally possible to land and walk out. Crossings less than 1/2 nm. except for very protected trips. | Crossings up to 2 nm. wide and/or fetches longer than 10 nm. | Crossings up to 5 nm. | Crossing more than 5 nm. but less than 3 hours' paddling time at the speed listed with the trip. Exposed ocean coasts are included when precautions are taken. | Trips combining a long fetch with stretches where a safe landing may be difficult or impossible for most of a day. |
| **Hydraulics** (Expected en route) kt. = knot | Insignificant currents | Max. predicted current up to 1 kt. | Max. predicted currents up to 2 kt. | Predicted currents may be more than 2 kt., but less than slowest paddler's top speed. | Currents may be faster than group can paddle against. | Exposure to hazards at any other levels taken to extremes. |
| **Route** | | Day trips near shore | Either has protection or intermittent places to get out. | May involve crossing eddy lines and tide rips. | May cross *strong* eddy lines, tide rips, and upswellings. | May include landing and launching in surf. | |
| **Acceptable Conditions** (No guarantees) | Calm | Generally try to avoid choppy water and/or winds above 10 kt. | Generally will not start out in whitecaps, but be prepared for paddling into waves large enough to wash over the deck and be comfortable paddling in at least 10 kt. winds. | May include steep waves and swells. Be comfortable paddling in 15 kt. winds. | For groups prepared to *knowingly* set out in rough weather, whitecaps, and fast currents. | May only be negotiable with favorable conditions. Kayak rescues may not be possible. |
| **Skills and Conditions** (The skills and experience required are cumulative with ascending levels.) | Ability to swim. Except with the leader's permission: (a) previous experience is required on trips more than 5 nm.; and (b) previous practice capsizing and wet exiting (or be willing to learn how before the trip.) | Participants must have practiced assisted sea kayak rescue techniques. | Conditions may require bracing skills. Previous group and self-rescue practice (both as rescuer and rescuee). | Conditions may require anticipatory leaning, reflexive bracing, using the paddle-to-stern stroke, the rudder, and the ability to read moving water. Familiarity with charts and navigation. | Trip members must have tested their skills in rough conditions, know their limits, and be self-reliant in the event of separation from the group. The ability to Eskimo roll is highly recommended as conditions can make sea kayak recues difficult. Rescue practice with the kayak and equipment used on this trip. | Extensive experience and skill including kayak surfing and rolling are required. |

popularity of the kayak coincides with a decline in the resource known as wilderness; big water, and the ocean in particular, is vast and the coastlines so extensive that the kayaker's environment represents a virtual last frontier for the wanderer.

Which reminds me of a trip my wife and I took kayaking up the Kona Coast of the Big Island of Hawaii. Here, on a coast dotted with hundred-million-dollar hotels, each protecting their miserable little beaches, we were able to land elsewhere on white sand beaches stretching for a mile without a single footprint. We saw almost no recreational boats along the coast, and upon our arrival in the lagoon for one of the luxury hotels, the gawking tourists either mistook us for part of the hotel pageantry (like the evening hula show) or were getting their first clue that the world was round.

Let's assume that finding your own wilderness to explore is an ultimate goal. Initially, though, you will probably gravitate, and wisely so, toward what I call "organized" wilderness. Usually these are areas that have been set aside, designated, protected, or otherwise developed—or possibly not developed—so that they lend themselves to exploration and camping by means of small boats. If you are a canoe camper it is inconceivable that you would not be familiar with the Boundary Waters Canoe Area, for example. Similarly, sea kayakers soon learn about certain areas that lend themselves naturally to being, and have been anointed accordingly as, sea-kayaking destinations. We list a number of those later in the chapter.

Often, such areas have had to be "organized" through volunteerism and political activism. Waterfront property is scarce, and coastal kayakers who wish to haul their boats out on a nice scenic beach are competing with persons who would like to own and "lock up" such spots for them-

selves, with developers who believe such a spot would offer a high return on investment if only a six-hundred-room high rise could be perched thereon, or perhaps with some governmental agency that deems their prize beach to be the only habitat of the neon-bellied oyster catcher—thus kayakers may be greeted with a NO LANDINGS PERMITTED sign. Needless to say, the organized areas that currently exist or are in the process of being assembled (for example, the Cascadia Marine Trail in the Pacific Northwest and the Maine Island Trail) are valuable indeed. Such organized areas are a good choice for you in your early explorations. These areas are also the likely venues for the packaged or outfitted tours.

## RIVERS, LAKES, AND OCEANS
### Rivers

Sadly, the number of rivers in the contiguous forty-eight states that offer the possibility of more than an overnight trip is a precious few. Some of these are big western whitewater rivers, most of which require permits, and many are renowned for their whitewater; these call for special skills. Yet rivers such as the upper Missouri and the Yellowstone, both in Montana, the Green in Utah and Colorado, and the desert rivers of eastern Oregon are worthy of research. Many waterways consisting of rivers and their impoundments (dams) could offer cruising and camping opportunities, but much of the challenge is finding suitable camping along these highly altered, in some cases heavily populated, waterways. The camping skills for this sort of adventure, which may be more akin to RV camping, are beyond the scope of this book.

Throughout Canada and in Alaska, there are

many rivers that over the years have attracted open canoes, but for many such trips a kayak would be perfectly suitable. However, even the largest kayaks lack the load capacity of a good expedition canoe, and if a trip in northern waters requires frequent or long portages, they would not be a good choice. Larger rivers such as the Mackenzie and the Yukon, on the other hand, would be fine waters for a kayak, and there are many northern rivers that typically expand into huge lakes along their course. Here the kayaker might find that on the big lake expansions the kayak is preferable to a canoe. Although camping skills along a river are not much different from those required in an ocean environment, river-running skills are certainly different. If you plan to head down-river in your kayak, make sure you acquire the necessary skills.

## Lakes

The kayak is the perfect craft for big-lake cruising and camping. For chains of lakes, where portages between lakes are required, the kayak seems less well suited; that's because loading and unloading a kayak is a cumbersome process compared with the open canoe, where you may have only two or three large packs; moreover, a canoe is designed to be carried. Cruising big lakes is not much different from ocean and coastal cruising, without the tides, currents, and salt. Except for very large bodies of water such as the Great Lakes or the Northwest Territories' Great Slave Lake, swell is not normally a factor, but wind on a big lake can be just as much a concern as it is in any coastal environment. Large shallow lakes—Manitoba's Lake Winnipeg, for example—are subject to violent wave action due to the buildup of wind energy over shallow water. Impoundments, where winds may

A Kayak camp. Note the Crazy Creek chair in front.

be funneled up valleys or between canyon walls, can also create wild water to rival the roughest storm-driven ocean environment. The arms of Yellowstone Lake, for example, are subject to fierce afternoon convection winds. But the kayak, due to its reduced windage, is certainly a more suitable craft for big lakes and troubled water than a canoe. Rough water is also caused by lots of motorboat traffic; here again, most people are going to feel more comfortable in a kayak. The popularity of the sea kayak has opened up a whole range of long-overlooked camping opportunities on big lakes. Lake Superior is a lake to be reckoned with no matter what kind of boat you are in, but such inland oceans have become much more attainable destinations with the advent of the modern kayak.

## Oceans

Unquestionably, this has been the focus of most of the action in sea kayaking, and it's the emphasis of this book. Oceans and coastlines may be the last wilderness. If you use the volume of guidebook material as a measure, it is clear that North America's inland waterways have been well cataloged compared with the availability of guidebooks for coastal areas. The phenomenon is like mountain biking: How many backroads and trails went to nowhere in obscurity before being "discovered" by the mountain bikers? Now, every mountain town and hamlet has its own mountain-bike guide. Sea kayaking still has a way to go. The latest edition of *Wilderness Waterways*, a bibliography of thousands of source materials for paddling, lists over 465 guidebooks in print; only 15 of those are for coastal areas (these are listed in the Appendix).

Herein lies the greatest challenge for the newcomer to coastal kayaking and camping. Those few areas that have been discovered and documented are in danger of being loved to death as kayakers flock to them. At this writing, one of those areas—the Broken Island group on Vancouver Island, off British Columbia's coast—is about to institute a permit system to control group size and campsite availability. Those areas that have not been discovered and cataloged present problems of access and egress within the bounds of knowing what is public, what is private, and equally important, what the hazards for a particular

route or area may be. Of course, there will be a certain number of you who, after mastering the paddling, navigation, and camping skills, will eschew the organized areas or the areas featured in guidebooks and magazine articles and undertake your own expedition planning. The research required to plan such a trip will become as much a part of the challenge as the actual execution. Such a trip is probably the dream come true, more likely the unfulfilled fantasy, of most of us who venture forth in our kayaks.

# AMERICAN DESTINATIONS

Here's just a sampling of areas around the map, including Hawaii, Canada, Alaska, and Mexico. These are not recommendations so much as an indicator of the huge menu of possible kayak camping destinations. You'll want to do more specific research: Charts, guidebooks, magazine articles, and state and provincial tourist bureaus can help pin down your own trip. (The entries in this section are courtesy of *Kayak Touring* magazine, 1994 edition.)

## Eastern Penobscot Bay, Maine

Offering fairly protected waters, Penobscot Bay is an ideal touring spot for kayakers. The eastern end, with its numerous accessible islands and pink granite beaches, is picturesque. Historically, the granite has been used to build cities such as New York and Washington, D.C. A few of the quarries are still actively mined today. A number of small islands (mostly private but accessible by joining the Maine Island Trail Association) can be reached from the Muscle Ridge Channel. And Stonington, a real working village, makes a convenient put-in.

## Casey Key, Florida

Part of the appeal of Casey Key, located in the Gulf Intracoastal Waterway between Sarasota and Fort Myers, is a pair of resident dolphins. Most days before noon, the dolphins will circle boats, seeking handouts, about a quarter mile offshore, so the early kayaker has the best chance of witnessing their antics. Every once in a while, migratory schools of dolphins will pass through, leaving behind the loyal two. Paddlers will also see osprey, eagles, and herons flitting among the mangrove shores and oyster bars.

## Wilderness Waterway, Florida

This is a wilderness waterway, a one-hundred-mile-long route through the Ten Thousand Islands for self-propelled craft and small boats marked out by the National Park Service between Everglades City and Flamingo. You'll paddle through a maze of channels, camp on sites two thousand years old, and see wildlife a paddle-length away. The route, part of Everglades National Park, leads through mangrove jungles described by an early visitor as "so thick a rabbit could scarcely pass through." Alligators shun the brackish waters, but expect hordes of wading birds, pelicans, and eagles. December through April is the best time to visit, and low bug season.

## Apostle Islands, Wisconsin

Trek to the northernmost point in Wisconsin, and launch into the twenty-two islands grouped off Bayfield Peninsula. Part of the mainland shore and twenty-one of the islands are within the Apostle Islands National Lakeshore. Oak Island is the highest, with a great view from the eastern sandstone heights, while Devil's Island is pocked with sea caves. Take note: This is Lake Superior and weather conditions can be intimidating.

## Rainy Lake, Voyageurs National Park, Minnesota

The numbers are incredible: 2,500 miles of shoreline and 1,600 islands crammed into a lake 60 miles long and 12 miles wide at its widest. It is Rainy Lake, the heart of Voyageurs National Park on the Minnesota-Ontario border just west of the Boundary Waters Canoe Area. Dozens of narrow coves and hidden bays are carved into the shoreline, and polished rock slabs smoothed by ancient glaciers lure sunbathers and offer prime picnic spots. Rainy is aligned along the path of the prevailing north winds, so beware of waves building up along the length of the lake and crashing on unprotected shores.

## Yellowstone Lake, Yellowstone National Park, Wyoming

Pack your long johns in your dry bag, load up with more color film than you think you can shoot, and enjoy the solitude of Yellowstone Lake in the heart of the Rocky Mountains. That's right, solitude. Launch your kayak into this 136-square-mile mini-ocean a mile and a half above sea level after Labor Day, and you'll have the three remote southern arms of the lake (open only to self-propelled craft and wilderness hikers) to yourself. The resonating bugle of a bull elk fractures the crystal air, flotillas of ducks cruise along the shores, geese wing overhead, and you could well spot a white pelican. Days should be on the cool side of crisp, but the threat of an early snowstorm or high winds hangs over the lake as fall slips away—so be forewarned.

## Gulf Islands, British Columbia

Just north of the United States' San Juans lie Canada's Gulf Islands, beautiful and ideal for kayak touring. Unlike the San Juans, where the water remains cold, the Gulf Islands form a basin, trapping the water and heating it all summer. The waters in this area are calm and protected, with only mild currents within the arms of the circling islands (passes into the adjoining Strait of Georgia are another story). From Galiano Island, a kayaker can explore any of more than two hundred islands, taking short two-day trips or longer journeys of a week or more. The most popular paddling time is May through September, but the weather usually remains promising throughout the year. Seals, otters, and an occasional whale are common sights.

## Vitus Lake and Port Valdez, Alaska

Kayak touring in Alaska is always an adventure, especially for those interested in glaciation. Following the shoreline out of Valdez, paddlers eventually reach a set of islands called the Valdez Keys. Observe seals, sea otters, diving ducks, eagles, and migrating birds passing through the area, or take day trips to different tidewater glaciers. Vitus Lake is home to the Bering Glacier, the world's fastest-surging glacier. After retreating for the past twenty years or so, the Bering Glacier has been rapidly advancing, more than a mile during last August alone. Paddle into Shoup Bay (a state park) on the north side of Port Valdez for a glimpse of mountain goats on the uplands, as well as a look at seventeen-mile-long Shoup Glacier,

which comes near the shore. Another tidewater glacier in the area, the Columbia, is calving so frequently it's difficult to approach. For the adventurous, catch an Alaska Ferry (one of the blue canoes) for the seven-hour ride from Whittier to Valdez, and then paddle the 140-odd miles back.

## Angel Island, San Francisco Bay

About three miles from the Marin Headlands in San Francisco Bay lies Angel Island, its wooded shores and isolated beaches visible from Sausalito but accessible only by small craft. Kayakers can enjoy the protected waters around the island or trade in their paddles to hike and mountain-bike on land.

## Magdalena Bay, Baja California, Mexico

This is a hundred-mile finger of water tucked in behind a barrier chain of desert islands down Baja California's Pacific coast. The mangrove estuaries, lagoons, and beaches are perfect for camping, as well as for watching the gray whales that congregate here in the hundreds between December and March. You may share prime whale-watching areas with a host of guided tours.

## Little Na Pali Coast, Hawaii

White sand beaches, rugged lava points, warm water—what sounds inviting in the summer turns into a description of paradise once the mercury starts to shrink on the mainland. While the north coast of Kauai—the true Na Pali Coast—is one of the world's prime sea-kayaking destinations in the summer, the protected southern coastline is a winter treat.

## Lake Powell, Utah

Lake Powell, the 140-mile-long impoundment of the Colorado River upstream from the Grand Canyon, calls for a day's float—or a year's exploration. Cruise through over one hundred major canyons and countless smaller ones— stark, deep gouges carved into the sandstone, soaring cliffs, incredible arches, and skylines notched like castles. Half-millennium-old Anasazi ruins dot Escalante, Lake, Mosqui, Navajo, and Reflection canyons. Many of the gorges hold petroglyphs. This is a high-use recreation lake, but you can find solitude in the smaller, more remote canyons. Late spring and early fall offer the best paddling.

# HOW TO PLAN A TRIP

If you don't already have a general geographic area in mind, just look at your world atlas. If time and money are no object, and you own or plan to acquire a folding kayak, then the world is your oyster. Less ambitious, and less expensive, options are usually much closer to home, especially if you live near the coast or the Great Lakes. Most often, people get their inspiration for kayak destinations from books, magazine articles, friends, a club newsletter, or perhaps a slide show put on by members of their local paddling club. An article in a generalized publication, such as *National Geographic*, might inspire you to travel to New Zealand, but you will be more likely to find specific information on paddling opportunities in New Zealand by reading one of the periodicals that specialize in canoeing and kayaking. It is customary for destination articles in such magazines to include a resource sidebar containing information on access, public transportation, camping and permits, pertinent agencies (as in national or provincial parks), and applicable charts or guidebooks. Check the outfitter or adventure paddling directories in these magazines to see where the popular destinations are. Use back issues of magazines to find destinations that may attract fewer folks than ones that have just been written up in *Canoe & Kayak,* for example.

In the Appendix of this book, we include several listings: periodicals, clubs, guidebooks, map sources, and parks. Another useful publication (from which many of the entries for the Appendix were extracted) is *Wilderness Waterways*, a whole water catalog. The guidebooks-in-print sections contain almost five hundred entries. There are pages of map sources, state and provincial agencies, videos and books, and countless other entries to aid you in basic research.

The best sources of all, however, are paddling friends or club members who have taken a trip recently. Plugging yourself into a network of paddlers will keep you abreast of what's really hot and what's not. Sometimes, the guidebooks, and especially magazine articles that resulted from all-expense-paid junkets for a writer, may not be entirely forthcoming or objective about an area. From paddlers whom you know (and, hopefully, who know you) you can learn about an area, warts and all. Important information concerning access, launch areas, stress-free landing areas for camping, water sources, and potential problem spots is best obtained from knowledgeable paddlers who have recently visited an area. On a trip to the Bella Bella area on the central British Columbia coast, our group carried charts with the combined notations of three separate parties who had made the trip during the previous three years. When two persons agreed that Island "X" was a four-star camping spot, we knew we had a winner.

## When to Go

When you go is an important consideration. Long weekends around summer holidays will almost guarantee that you'll be competing for space on the road and on the water. The midsummer months bring forth like-minded outdoor travelers, and you'll have to be extremely clever or lucky to avoid traffic jams in the popular areas. During such times, there's a simple formula for finding solitude: The harder you work, the more you'll get. Driving a hundred miles of dirt road, carrying your boat a mile to the water, paddling out through and landing in surf zones, making a two-hour channel crossing—these are some of the ways to put distance between you and the crowd. If you can drive to the launch area on a freeway and launch on a quiet beach, you'll have plenty of company. Needless to say, midweek departures, off-season itineraries, and less accessible launch sites will tend to give you more living space—if that's what you seek.

For novice kayak campers, the more popular destinations may provide a comfort or security factor. You may, in fact, wish to mingle with seafarers who are out there for many of the same reasons you are (solitude not being one of them). Some of our most enjoyable trips have been in heavily trafficked areas, at high season, where we shared campsites with many neighbors.

That's part of the planning. Are you looking for a wilderness or semiwilderness experience, or will you be just as happy sharing the water and the campsites with other like-minded people?

## Whom to Go With

So now you've identified an area. Your choice of destination will have to take into consideration the amount of time available and the people. Planning a solo trip is infinitely easier than orga-

nizing a group of six persons. Avoid groups larger than six; coordinating the wishes, wants, physical and emotional capabilities, and personal chemistry of large groups destroys the real reason for going kayak camping: to get away from it all. Equally important, there are very few coastal areas where you can accommodate large parties without straining the resources and adversely affecting the environment. At the other extreme, solo voyaging is not recommended for any but the most skilled and self-reliant; such persons should know their capabilities and themselves exceedingly well. For a group, knowing each person's capabilities is extremely important. It's a gross oversimplification, but planning a trip around the weakest crew member and the longest exposed crossing is a good way to increase the fun and stay out of trouble. Consider, as well, the mix of capabilities. One weak paddler in a group of six strong paddlers may be acceptable; two weak paddlers in a group of four could be a drag.

## How Much, How Far?

Time is even more valuable than money. We're often lucky to be able to carve out a week's vacation. Taking an overnight trip or a long weekend is one way we pack some outdoor living into our busy schedules, and such jaunts are probably desirable as shakedown cruises before we embark on a more extended expedition. Keep in mind, however, that the "fiddle-to-fun" factor can get out of kilter. You'll need to assemble virtually all of the same boating and camping components for a three-day trip as you would for a month-long expedition. Only the food quantities change. Large groups take longer to organize and outfit, and the itinerary unfolds (except for the most seasoned campers who have functioned together before) at the pace of the slowest member. Consider, also, how far you wish to drive—or fly, or ferry, or walk—relative to your time on the water. Ten hours of driving to do a three-day trip seems like a lousy ratio.

It's easy to look at the state or provincial road map, or even the detailed charts, and visualize an itinerary that gobbles up vast areas of coastline or island archipelagos. Too much time spent on freeways and jet airplanes has warped our sense of human-powered distances. Most people will find that ten miles in a kayak is a long day, and that's assuming that fair weather and fair winds prevail. It's not uncommon for seasoned expeditioners to cover distances of twenty, even thirty miles a day, but even under ideal paddling conditions, a major limiting factor is how long you are able to sit on your butt in a tiny cockpit! Plan on cruising at no more than three knots. Rest stops, adverse winds, a weak paddler—any or all of these factors can quickly reduce progress to two knots. Consider the difference between these two speeds: At three knots a twelve-mile distance is covered in four hours; at two knots, a fanny-numbing six hours! On the other hand, a solo paddler, or strong twosome (especially if they're in a double kayak) might easily plan their trip around a four-knot pace. It's best to be conservative in the coastal environment. Seemingly small differences in speed can make a huge difference in the number of hours you're confined to your boat. Which brings us to another major consideration.

## Planning Accordingly

Audrey Sutherland, a durable woman and peripatetic kayaker, has written widely and speaks often at sea-kayak symposia on the subject of camping. She has made the following unscientific, but probably accurate, observation:

Kayakers spend an average of two hours to make, and two hours to break, camp. A trip plan that calls for making and breaking camp each day, or even every other day, means that as many as four hours will be spent in loading and unloading the kayaks, setting up and taking down the camp. Expeditions and itineraries covering long distances from point to point need to be planned accordingly; you'll pack lighter, and meals must be arranged to minimize preparation time. Small, experienced, lightly outfitted groups should be able to cut that average time in half.

People looking for a more relaxed mode of kayak touring should consider the base-camp approach, or in the case of a longer trip, a series of base camps. In view of the inordinate amount of time, and physical effort, that must be devoted to making and breaking camp, it makes sense to paddle twelve miles in one day (four hours on the water) and spend two or three days at one site, rather than to cover the same distance in two days, and have to set and break two camps.

Larger groups, and especially ones that include several novice campers, may want to consider a base camp—period. The idea here is to find a pleasant campsite from which you may launch day trips. The energetic and adventurous members of the party can launch day trips from the base camp, then return each day to a camp that becomes increasingly more comfortable. Others will simply wish to stay in camp and read, work on their tans, cook, or go for a hike. The base-camp approach is a good way to accommodate a wide variety of skill and energy levels. A plea: There may be many popular areas where your extended stay at one camp may limit others' ability to enjoy the same site. Here's a good time to observe the Golden Rule. A three- or four-day limit seems reasonable in areas of high traffic and limited sites.

# BOATS FOR EXPEDITIONS (NEAR AND FAR)

## KAYAK TYPES

The subject of hull design is covered in many other kayaking books, and there is no need to duplicate much of that excellent information. For our purposes, we need to distinguish between whitewater kayaks, multipurpose kayaks, and so-called sea kayaks, and recognize as well that a boat that can perform well in one set of conditions (a big piece of open water) may not perform so well in another (river rapids). From time to time, any boat may be called upon to perform in waters for which it is not optimally designed. You, the operator, will have to make up for any deficiency. Since we are planning to go camping, we are interested in boats that have enough carrying capacity to carry us and all of the gear that we feel is necessary for our comfort and safety. (Chapter 10, "Self-Support River Running," will examine a few whitewater boats and their capacity to absorb a minimalist outfit.) Different folks will have very different ideas about what it takes to be comfortable in the out-of-

doors. We talked about the minimalist and the gear hog in Chapter 1, and focused primarily on the subject of capacity. Here we'll look at a few specific boats, some of the features that either do or don't lend themselves to a particular style of camping, and a number of attributes that can make a difference in your trip.

### Skinny Little Boats

A lot of people like these because they cut through the water quickly and respond nicely to every stroke nuance, and because they represent a pure, yet elegant, approach to an elegant pastime. Some of these same people thought that car evolution started to go downhill—became too comfortable—after the Austin Healey and Morgan Plus Four went out of production. Boats like the Valley Canoe Products, Nordkapp series, Anas Acutas, and Pintail are in this category; likewise, the Necky Arluck 1.8, Current Designs Solstice SS, the Pacific Water Sports Seal, and other boats that seem to be around

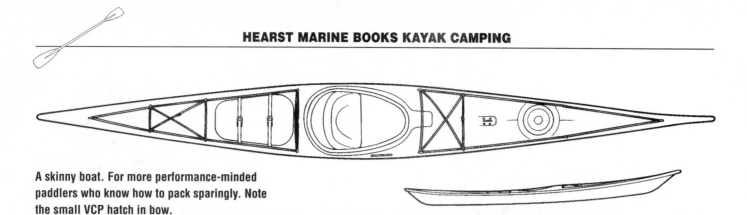

A skinny boat. For more performance-minded paddlers who know how to pack sparingly. Note the small VCP hatch in bow.

twenty-one inches wide would compare. Most are long-nosed and shallow in depth. Reading Chapter 10 on self-support river running might be helpful, as most of these skinny boats demand self-discipline when it comes to your food and gear. The skinny boats are characterized by small hatches, and a popular style is the VCP, a seven-inch-diameter hole over which is fitted a semihard rubber gasket cover. The small diameter limits the size of gear you can fit in, but the small opening and tight gasket closure also mean that you can risk cramming in food, clothing, even a sleeping bag, and not necessarily have to use a waterproof enclosure for the gear. Some skinny boats (and a few others) employ a screw (or Thompson) hatch. It's not really for loading gear, but permits loading gear through the cockpit in a nonbulkheaded kayak; the hole serves as a way of maneuvering the gear as it works its way toward the peaked bow. If you choose or find yourself with one of these boats, attach a trailing string to the gear that's destined for the boat peak so you can pull it out (and everything you stuffed in behind it) at landing time.

If you are new to the sport, don't dismiss the skinny boats on the basis of this seemingly lighthearted analysis. The reality for most people is that they take short camping trips and they probably need only half of what they take. Skinny boats are fun to paddle, and for all those outings when you are not camping, you'll be enjoying the sport at its most exhilarating. And keep in mind that some notable long-distance voyages have been made in these high-performance boats.

## Fat Boats

You'll never see them advertised that way. "High volume," "stable," "excellent family boat," and "great for photography and bird watching" are some of the popular phrases to describe the big boats. These station wagons have a

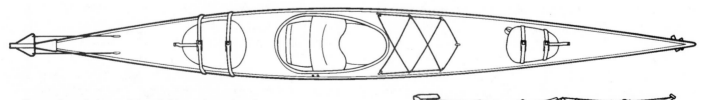

Somewhere between fat and skinny. A sea kayak is made in both plastic and fiberglass models, with length and volume suitable for a good-sized load and good hull speed.

beam of about twenty-four inches and are deep at the midsection. Not only do their high-peaked decks give you more space—there's room for a barbecue or a month's provisions—but in rough water you'll probably enjoy a drier ride. Kayaks like the Eddyline Wind Dancer, Pacific Water Sports Sea Otter, Necky Tesla, Easy Rider 17, and the eighteen-foot Eskimo are big, stable, and capable of handling a big load. If you are primarily interested in kayak camping, if you value comfort over speed or high performance and don't care if your boxcar is empty on all those day trips, go for a fat boat. When you do go camping, you'll appreciate not only the extra space, but the ease of loading. Big hatches also make loading easier, and bigger boats tend to have bigger hatches. Watertightness seems to suffer inversely with increasing hatch size. That's no big deal; packing virtually all of your gear in a waterproof, so-called dry bag is a good idea no matter what kind of boat you paddle. Large boats are also less sensitive to load placement (covered later in this chapter); there's less performance to begin with, hence less to degrade. A fat boat is also a wise choice if you want to share it with other friends or family members. A total novice can jump in and feel secure. A skinny boat will probably have a self-limiting usage.

## Special Boats

You will see boats—fat, skinny, and in between—advertised as "expedition outfitted." That can mean the addition of a rudder to a kayak that is available stripped at a very low price. It might also mean the addition of hatches, or bulkheads. I recognize that many expedition paddlers are happy (even happiest) in a boat with no rudder, but I will describe my version of the expedition or kayak-tripping ves-

sel: The boat is seventeen feet in length, or perhaps eighteen. The boat has high volume in the midsection, at least. Hatches are watertight or close to it. There are front and rear bulkheads. Gear-storage capacity behind the seat and in front of the foot pedals is ample (for those things you want to get at during the day). I consider a rudder a necessity. Deck lines running the length of the hull, bungees fore and aft of the cockpit, a recessed area for a deck-

**Taking the kids. This double kayak has a large center hatch.**

mounted compass, and provision for a self-rescue setup are there. The seat is comfortable and adjustable and the rudder foot controls are also easily adjustable while sitting in the boat. A paddle park is desirable. Hatches, in addition to being watertight, are easy to get into. The hatches and cargo areas are free of burrs, protruding screws, or other things that might poke holes in waterproof bags. Finally, and hardest to determine, the tripping boat, when heavily loaded, performs almost as well as when empty, possibly better.

As it turns out, many of the above attributes do not seem to apply to frame-and-fabric folding kayaks like the Klepper, Feathercraft, and Folboat. Yet these ingenious craft are the perfect vehicles for the kayak camper who has space constraints in storing a boat at home (like an apartment) or for folks who really plan to travel globally and require a boat they can transport on planes, large and small. Because of the internal frame systems, space in these boats is usually more constrained than in hard-shelled kayaks of comparable dimensions. Some of the packing strategies will be like those for skinny kayaks and whitewater kayaks. Watertight bulkheads are not the norm in folding kayaks, so everything must have its own fail-safe container.

In Chapter 2, the relative merits of single and double kayaks were discussed. Family kayakers may want to investigate doubles like the Eddyline San Juan, a very fat, stable boat with a center hatch that can be set up to accommodate a small child, or look into the availability of three-seaters; a few manufacturers are now offering these.

## PACKING A KAYAK

It's not uncommon to have a "packing party" before a trip. Your crew, consisting of three couples, is planning a two-week trip on the coast of Newfoundland. The boats will be two double kayaks and two singles. Two people are in charge of the food, another will honcho the gathering of some common items like kitchen hardware, the first-aid kit, water purifier, and the communal rain fly. Each person has to assemble his or her own clothing and personal gear, and gear hogs seem to outnumber minimalists in our hedonistic world. The packing party is a dress rehearsal in which you find out if all this stuff will really fit into four boats, plus water supplies, and also provides an opportunity for figuring out what goes where. Launch sites are often congested, tiny, precarious perches—like a small floating dock—and may be lashed by

weather on your launch day. They can be lousy places to practice loading a boat, especially if you find out that the two-burner stove won't fit into any of your kayaks! The same applies if you are a party of one.

Whatever you are taking, many small packs are preferable to a few large packs. You'll be able to utilize those funny-shaped spaces in the boat, and load distribution is more flexible. You want a kayak to be well trimmed (sit level in the water, rather than bow-heavy, stern-heavy, or tilted to one side), or you're going to have performance and control problems. To consolidate all those small packs for transport to and from your kayak at launches and landings, use large mesh bags which are lightweight, take up little space, and dry quickly.

A worthy method for organizing your load is to take all your gear and divide it into three piles: the items you must have, those that are desirable, and those that could be dispensed with. If you pack group one first, by the time you get to group three, you may decide that the backgammon set can stay home. Another plan (possibly superimposed on the first method) is

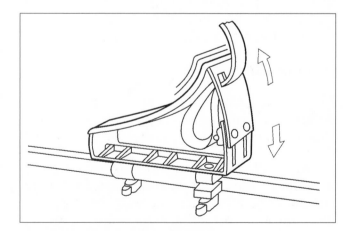

Cradles protect the hull from deforming.

**Kayaks on wheels boarding the Washington State Ferries.**

to make three piles organized by need to access. Extra clothing and the tent won't be needed until you get into camp, so you can safely bury them in the peak of your boat. Lunch, the first-aid kit, a water bottle, and your camera ought to be in the cockpit where you can get at them quickly. Likewise, don't bury the rain jacket, wool hat, and

gloves on a day when the weather might deteriorate rapidly. Think about a situation on open water when wind chill and wet might actually threaten your safety if you are unable to dress up for bad weather quickly.

There are a few other things to consider. As with a good shopping bag load, get the heavy stuff on the bottom, and then try to concentrate it toward the center of the boat (that's where your volume and buoyancy is). Distribute the load to achieve a level trim. If you've got a compass on deck, make sure that metallic items— an ax can throw your compass way out of whack—aren't creating compass deviation (simply, a wrong reading). Finally, keep deck clutter to a minimum. Bulky or heavy items can be wind catchers or upset the ideal of a low center of gravity. They can deflect waves into your

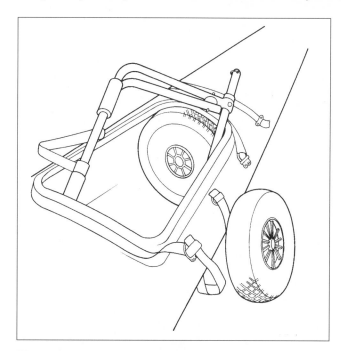

**Wheels are a nice option, especially if you use ferry-boat access or have a long distance between car and water.**

face, or they may come unstuck in rough water just when you need to be devoting all your attention to keeping the boat under control.

# TRANSPORTING A BOAT

Some of the most critical mileage for your kayak(s) is to and from the water. Thus you need a good set of racks for your vehicle. Two rack manufacturers, Thule and Yakima, make excellent systems, including solutions to the problem of rain-gutterless cars. Regardless of which system you choose (including home-built racks), you should have cradles into which you nest the kayak. Not only is your boat more secure, but you'll prevent hull deformation, even cracks, which can occur when boats are lashed to a flat rack. If you don't have cradles, consider a stacker bar; then load kayaks on their edges or gunwales where the seams create a thicker, stronger point of contact with the racks. Also, you can stack five kayaks side by side on a rack that might accommodate only two—at most, three—kayaks side by side in cradles.

In the majority of situations, you will drive to the launch point and carry your kayak on your shoulder, or double-team it with a friend, to the water. There are, however, many situations where you may have long distances from car to water, or where you need to transport your loaded—it's a floating backpack, remember—kayak to the water. There are more than a few kayaking destinations—like the Washington State Ferry system—where larger boats are part of the water-access plan. An unloaded kayak is merely awkward to carry for more than a short distance. A loaded kayak can ruin your back, if you and a friend can lift it at all. Consider wheels. There are several choices on the market, ranging from compact, lightweight models that can be easily stowed in a hatch when you get to the water, to all-terrain beasts that can roll over rocks, sand, grates, and gravel carrying a fully loaded double kayak. Unfortunately, wheels with the latter capability are likely to take up more hatch space—if they fit at all—than you can afford. We do picture one set of wheels that can transport a huge load and fold up to an acceptably compact package. You may never need a set of wheels, but most serious kayak campers, sooner or later, find them to be a necessity.

# CLOTHES FOR
# KAYAK CAMPERS

Only winter mountaineering rivals kayak camping as a challenge for figuring out the proper attire. We're amphibious, and our environment is hot and sunny one moment, cold and windy the next. If you shove off for a three-mile channel crossing in brilliant sunshine clad in your short-sleeve shirt, and the wind rises, bringing in a sea fog from offshore, you can't just stand up in your kayak and don a new outfit. The opposite scenario is almost as awkward. The overdressed cross-country skier who gets overheated after the first hundred yards can step off to the side of the trail and stuff his down parka back in his pack. Where are you going to stuff your hooded anorak and pile sweater in the same situation on the water? Like the skier, we are engaged in an aerobic activity, creating not only heat, but moisture in the form of sweat. When we stop paddling, perhaps to go ashore, a slight wind and evaporation of the sweat will have us shivering in moments.

Look at six sea kayakers on a trip and you'll see six different systems for dealing with these variables—or perhaps no system. That's because no one's really figured it out yet, and everybody's personal body thermostat and tolerance for suffering is different. Fortunately, modern technology has been brought to bear on fabrics, coatings, and fillings for outdoor garments to produce the equivalent of "smart" wear. Major companies have spent millions of dollars to develop specialized applications like Gore-Tex, Polartec, Thermoloft, Coolmax, Thermax, and Supplex to deal with conflicting variables; we want lightweight garments, but we want to stay warm (or cool) and dry. We want to keep water out, but we want moisture (sweat) to escape. We want to be windproof and waterproof, but we can't paddle all day in a sauna. If our clothes get wet (and this is a wet sport), we have to be able to dry them quickly.

Some of the old standbys acclaimed in early books on camping still work: cotton duck, wool, silk, down, and coated nylon. I still prefer wool to pile and am willing to suffer the slight weight penalty, but pile linings or synthetic fillings have mostly replaced down, especially for wet environments. Coated fabrics have been around for a while, and we all remember those early ones that started to flake and separate from the nylon after a year's hard use. Now, special and more durable coatings literally draw moisture out of a garment through molecular action. These coated fabrics compete with the new breed of laminated fabrics (the best

## WIND CHILL CHART

### Wind Temperature (Fahrenheit/Centigrade)

| (Miles per hour) (Kilometers per hour) | | | | | | | | | | | | | | |
|---|---|---|---|---|---|---|---|---|---|---|---|---|---|---|
| CALM | 35 | 30 | 25 | 20 | 15 | 10 | 5 | 0 | -5 | -10 | -15 | -20 | -25 | -30 |
| *CALM* | *27* | *-1* | | *-4* | | *-7* | | *-9* | | *-12* | | *-15* | | *-18* |
| | | *-21* | | *-23* | | *-26* | | *-29* | | *-32* | | *-34* | | |

### Equivalent Temperature (Fahrenheit/Centigrade)

| | 35 | 30 | 25 | 20 | 15 | 10 | 5 | 0 | -5 | -10 | -15 | -20 | -25 | -30 |
|---|---|---|---|---|---|---|---|---|---|---|---|---|---|---|
| 5 MPH | 33 | 27 | 21 | 16 | 12 | 7 | 1 | -6 | -11 | -15 | -20 | -26 | -31 | -35 |
| *8 KPH* | *1* | | *-3* | | *-6* | | *-9* | | *-11* | | *-14* | | *-17* | |
| *-21* | | *-24* | | *-26* | | *-29* | | *-32* | | *-35* | | *-37* | | |
| 10 MPH | 21 | 16 | 9 | 2 | -2 | -9 | -15 | -22 | -27 | -31 | -38 | -45 | -52 | -58 |
| *16 KPH* | *-6* | | *-9* | | *-13* | | *-17* | | *-19* | | *-23* | | *-26* | |
| *-30* | | *-33* | | *-35* | | *-39* | | *-43* | | *-47* | | *-50* | | |
| 15 MPH | 16 | 11 | 1 | -6 | -11 | -18 | -25 | -33 | -40 | -45 | -51 | -60 | -65 | -70 |
| *24 KPH* | *-9* | | *-12* | | *-17* | | *-21* | | *-24* | | *-28* | | *-32* | |
| *-36* | | *-40* | | *-43* | | *-46* | | *-51* | | *-54* | | *-57* | | |
| 20 MPH | 12 | 3 | -4 | -9 | -17 | -24 | -32 | -40 | -46 | -52 | -60 | -68 | -76 | -81 |
| *32 KPH* | *-11* | *-16* | | *-20* | | *-23* | | *-27* | | *-31* | | *-36* | | *-40* |
| *-43* | | *-47* | | *-51* | | *-56* | | *-60* | | *-63* | | | | |
| 25 MPH | 7 | 0 | -7 | -15 | -22 | -29 | -37 | -45 | -52 | -58 | -67 | -75 | -83 | -89 |
| *40 KPH* | *-14* | *-18* | | *-22* | | *-26* | | *-30* | | *-34* | | *-38* | | *-43* |
| *-47* | | *-50* | | *-55* | | *-59* | | *-64* | | *-67* | | | | |
| 30 MPH | 5 | -2 | -11 | -18 | -26 | -33 | -41 | -49 | -56 | -63 | -70 | -78 | -87 | -94 |

Reprinted with permission of the publisher from *Hypothermia, Frostbite & Other Cold Injuries* by James A. Wilkerson, Cameron Bangs, M.D., and John S. Hayward, Ph.D. Seattle: The Mountaineers.

known of these is Gore-Tex), which incorporate a membrane that also uses the pressure of water vapor (through body heat) to propel water molecules through the fabric. Forget the physics; the intended result is garments that are waterproof, yet breathable. Fabric technology and garment construction are changing almost as fast as computers; when you go shopping you'll want to look for garments made by reputable manufacturers employing the latest fabric technology, sold by a retailer who can explain "moisture vapor transpiration" so you'll understand it. But be forewarned: Some of these fabulous garments are not cheap.

Outdoor-wear technology may be changing rapidly, but some basic principles never change. Moisture evaporation from your skin will cool you down. The wind-chill factor is for real (see the chart). The greatest heat loss occurs through the head (as much as 60 percent), so if your feet are cold, put on a hat—no kidding! Avoid water-absorbing fabrics—cotton's the worst. Use layering so that you can don and doff layers as conditions change, or to create dead air space. Dead air space will provide warmth and its corollary, a medium to allow moisture evaporation away from the skin. Now we're back to this technology thing. You want hydrophobic materials next to your skin that will "wick" moisture away. A molecular scientist can perhaps explain to you how body heat can cause moisture to migrate to the outer layers of your garments. Once it gets to the outer layer, you want to avoid condensation; hence the advent of the so-called breathable fabrics.

Let's get away from science now for a bit and look at some actual pieces of clothing that are meant to keep you warm, dry, and comfortable. You also need to know how much to have of what.

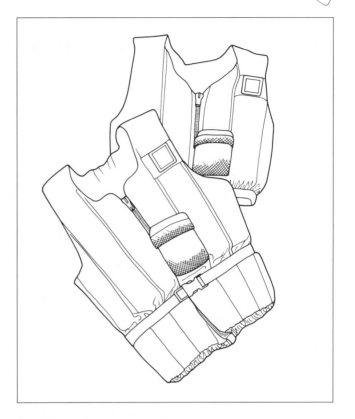

Shorty PFD (top) and PFD with cuff (bottom). They are for both flotation and thermal protection.

## SPECIAL CONSIDERATIONS FOR THE KAYAKER

Two essential pieces of kayaking equipment should be considered as part of your clothing: your PFD (life preserver) and spray skirt. Even in the first scenario at the start of this chapter, when you've set off in sunshine, in a T-shirt, and watched your day get unmade, you have some built-in protection. The PFD, usually made of fabric-covered foam blocks, is a thermal barrier—lots of dead air space—and when you pull up the tunnel of your spray skirt over the PFD and pull the drawstring

# SPECIAL CLOTHING CONSIDERATIONS FOR THE KAYAKER

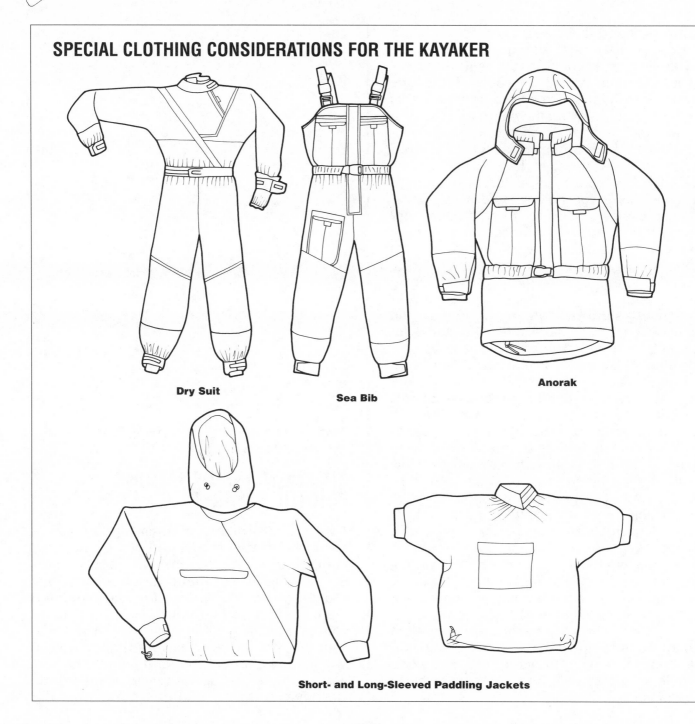

Dry Suit

Sea Bib

Anorak

Short- and Long-Sleeved Paddling Jackets

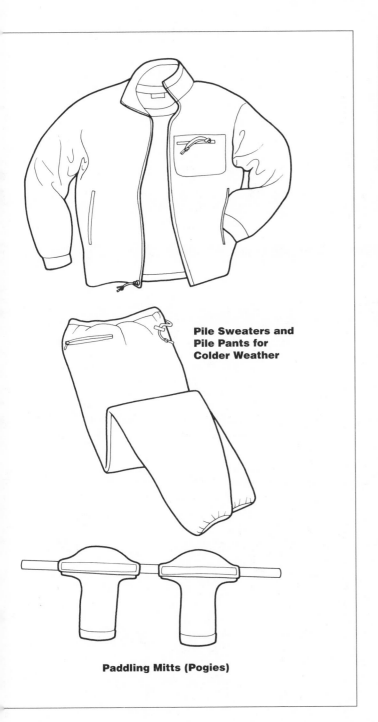

**Pile Sweaters and
Pile Pants for
Colder Weather**

**Paddling Mitts (Pogies)**

tight around the top, you've got the equivalent of half a down parka. Belowdecks, even in a pair of shorts, you are in a thermal cocoon. Only your arms, neck, and shoulders are at risk. This is a good reason to always have a warm hat—like a pile or wool ski hat—near at hand. Pull a lightweight—even short-sleeve—paddling jacket over you, and you can withstand some fairly drastic conditions.

About that thermal vest, your PFD. Onshore, put your rain jacket or anorak over top, and you've created a huge reservoir of dead air and warmth potential. But consider the following caution based only on anecdotal evidence: On the water, the PFD should not be worn under the paddling jacket or anorak. In a capsize, the water can quickly find its way into that dead air space, turning you into a water-filled Michelin Man and offsetting the buoyancy of the PFD.

Here's a dressing sequence that will keep you warm and dry in a broad range of conditions: from the inside out, a polypropylene (or any hydrophobic, synthetic material, such as Capilene, Thermax, etc.) long- or short-sleeve shirt, short-sleeve water-resistant paddling jacket, the PFD, and the spray skirt. If you are setting out in wet and windy weather—or know it's coming—consider a more defensive system: polypro long-sleeve shirt, light pile sweater, spray skirt, anorak or paddling jacket, and PFD. Now, you can pull the waist of your paddling jacket down over the tunnel of the spray skirt. Pull the drawstring tight and you are a fortress. And don't forget the hat and mitts.

Almost as important as your head are your hands—maybe more so. They are a crucial component in your transmission system. Your hands will get wet. Drip rings are a great way to reduce the flow of water back and forth on your paddle shaft (and over your digits), but even a light breeze can convert damp hands into para-

# FOOTWEAR

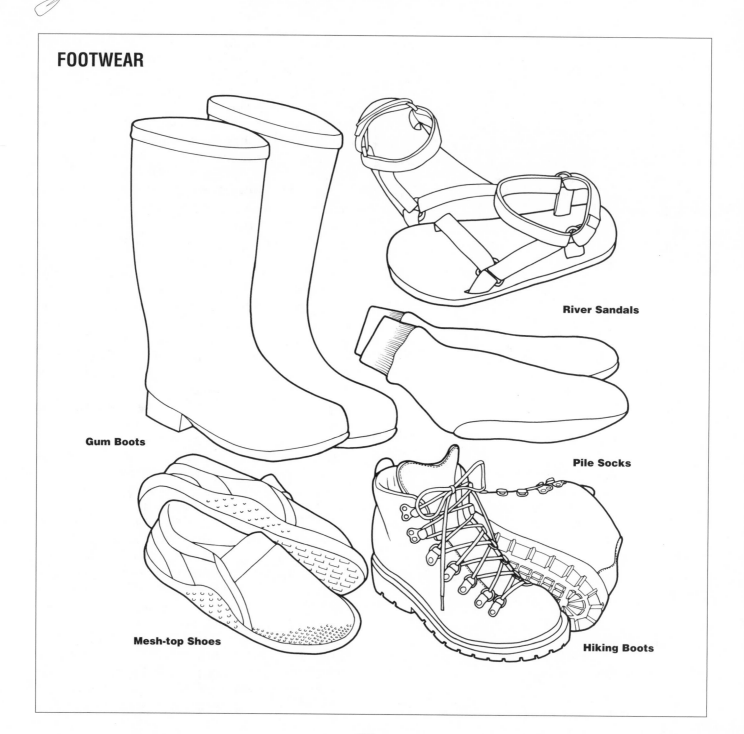

River Sandals

Gum Boots

Pile Socks

Mesh-top Shoes

Hiking Boots

lyzed claws. Paddle mitts should be in every kayak tripper's close-at-hand gear bag. These may be gloves of rubber, wool, or neoprene, or consider the special "Pogies" which attach to the paddle shaft so that you can hold the bare paddle shaft while your hands and wrists are completely covered.

What about belowdecks? You can paddle in shorts in all but winter weather if you have a good secure spray skirt, but your choice of pants may be more related to conditions when you exit your kayak than to those on the water. Also, every time you undo your spray skirt—unless you are scrupulously fastidious—you get some water in the boat or on the seat. For this reason many kayakers will wear polypropylene long johns, rain pants, or, at a miminum, pants of a fast-drying fabric like Supplex. For cold, wet conditions, a pair of pile pants makes for very comfortable paddling. Whatever you wear below the waist, be wary of belts, rivets, suspender buttons, or the like that are going to poke you in the lower back while sitting in those form-fitting seats. Take your change and wallet out of your pockets, too. They're worse than having a stone in your shoe.

So that's what you'll look like on the water. What about the amphibious you?

## THE REST OF THE OUTFIT

In his classic work on canoe camping, *North American Canoe Country*, Calvin Rutstrum suggested that the clothing pack consist of a change of underwear and six pairs of socks. If you think that's just some hair-shirted old north-woodsman's view, listen to Audrey Sutherland, a petite kayaker with as impressive a résumé of exploration by paddle as Rutstrum's: "What do you really need? What you wear on the plane or car en route to the launch spot, what you wear in the boat, and your rain gear. You only need that much plus two extra pairs of socks, and one extra set of underwear." Rutstrum is apparently less willing to do as much laundry as Sutherland. Rutstrum's theory, and it's a good one, is that no matter how rough the going gets, even if the rest of your outfit is caked in grime and grit, simply putting on a fresh pair of socks is the next best thing to a hot shower.

So let's talk socks. Wool rag socks are my first choice. Even wet they'll keep your feet warm. They provide a nice cushion inside any pair of boots, and you can get several days' wear out of them unless you go over your boots in bog mud. They can be worn in any style of boot, or in sandals. For those who have had an aversion to wool since childhood, there are now pile socks on the market. Pile seems to have most of the warm-when-wet, cushionlike attributes of wool, except that salt water gives them a sticky feel that I find annoying. The next choice would be thin polypropylene (or similar hydrophobic synthetic) socks, which are best for folks who choose neoprene or wet-suit booties for footwear. Wear them inside the booties and wash them out regularly to mitigate the inevitable "bootie breath" which results from the migration of sweat into the neoprene.

Recent entries into the sock derby are waterproof socks called Seal Skinz from Du Pont. You wear a thin polypro liner inside. Although pricey, the system seems to be a real breakthrough in outdoor comfort—especially in the kayaker's environment.

Forget cotton socks, period.

In fact, forget cotton. Cotton T-shirts are to bureaus what diapers are to landfills. We all have a ton of them, but unless you are kayaking in the desert they have a negative clothing value. Cotton has an affinity—as opposed to a phobia—for water and salt. Once the salt invades, any cotton garment becomes a moisture magnet—literally condensing moisture out of the atmosphere to keep you damp on even a warm, dry day. That said, I took a kayak trip in the tropics some years back and a T-shirt was my only garment (other than a bathing suit). If the spray didn't keep it damp, I'd dip it in the ocean. As the moisture evaporated, I enjoyed the natural refrigeration. That's exactly the opposite of your goal in the temperate and northerly zones. Back in the real world, surprisingly, there are some cotton twills and cotton/synthetic blends that do a nice job in the kayaker's environment because there is no nap and the fabric dries quickly. If you must take a cotton T-shirt, wear it only in your sleeping bag and don't let it out of your pack or tent.

Cotton undershorts are almost as useless as cotton T-shirts. Consider nylon running shorts instead. In hot weather they can be your only pants, in or out of the kayak. As underpants, they are hydrophobic and fast drying. Wear them when you bathe under the solar shower (covered in Chapter 6) and you take care of the modesty thing while laundering them. A few minutes in the breeze and you can put another pair of pants on over them if the weather is cool. Under a pair of pile pants, your damp shorts will finish drying in moments.

# FOOTWEAR

Three pairs of footwear will cover every contingency; in warm weather you might get away with two. If you are on a real space diet and hikes on land are short and sweet, just a pair of gum boots could suffice. In warm weather, a pair of river sandals can be worn in the boat and you're never constrained about jumping out of the kayak into the water as you launch and land your

**CLOTHING LIST**

- rain jacket or anorak
- rain pants or sea bib
- wool or pile ski hat
- mitts or Pogies
- sandals
- gum boots
- 2 pairs heavy wool socks per week
- 1 long-sleeve polypro (or comparable) shirt
- 1 short-sleeve polypro (or comparable) shirt
- pile sweater
- pile pants
- 2 pairs nylon running shorts
- fast-drying shorts or long pants
- cotton T-shirt for sleeping
- towel (not clothing, but usually gets packed in the clothing bag)

boat; then, they're great for beachcombing. Lightweight, low-top hiking shoes—even running shoes—give you footwear for hiking.

In all but the most benign weather, I wouldn't be without a pair of knee-high gum boots. Worn in the boat, they allow for a dry launch and landing (if you pay attention!), and unlike in sandals, you can tromp around in clay, mud, cobble, gravel, and other combinations of slime without paranoia. If you are in shorts, or care to hike up your long pants, you might prefer cooler, lighter footwear, like the mesh-top, rubber-soled "socks" now marketed by some footwear companies. They keep out sand and gravel better than sandals, and though your feet may be wet and cold for a short time, they do dry out quickly.

Some kayakers favor neoprene booties. These are a good choice for whitewater kayakers, but have limitations for the touring paddler.

They are always damp, hold an odor like a grudge, and make for lousy hiking or camping boots when you get on land. They are an alternative to the gum boots, but seem to offer no advantages.

# RAINWEAR

Buy the best you can afford. The rain-suit top should be your paddling jacket or anorak as well. The jacket's value as wind protection is as important as for rain repellency. A hooded jacket is best if you want to wear a peaked (baseball style) hat or toque. If you favor a sou'wester or brimmed hat, a nonhooded jacket might be best. Remember, breathability is important, since you'll be generating plenty of heat as you paddle. Rain pants or a sea bib are also a must. Toss a coin to decide whether your pants should be tucked in or left outside your boots. A broad-brimmed rain hat is my choice, because it leaves my peripheral vision intact, but well-designed paddling jackets have hoods designed to minimize tunnel vision, and a baseball-style hat will keep the hood from drooping over your eyes.

# FINDING AND MAKING CAMP

## ORGANIZED AREAS

Almost by definition, finding and making camp in an organized area is a matter of following directions. Such areas include national and provincial parks, state or intracoastal water trails, or areas managed by such diverse agencies as the BLM (Bureau of Land Management), state DNR (Department of Natural Resources), U.S. Forest Service, fish and wildlife departments, and even combinations of agencies. Some areas are described in elaborate and detailed brochures; they may require registration and permits, and there may or may not be a fee for camping; such areas may or may not have regulations posted at access points. Most organized areas, by this time, have been detailed in a guidebook (see the Appendix), and you shouldn't leave home without one. From either a guidebook or from area-provided literature, you need to know, at a minimum, the locations of designated campsites, the locations of places where you are not welcome, and the litany of

dos and don'ts for the area: for example, whether open fires are permitted or not permitted, tideland and/or upland restrictions, and any restrictions regarding overnight camping or day use, shellfish harvesting, wildfowl nesting seasons, water potability, or group size.

The main problem for those of us who tour and camp in the organized areas is that they are often intertwined with private lands. "Water trails" are more like airspace than railroad tracks. It's your job to gather the facts and know where you can go and what's permitted, which is akin to filing a flight plan in order to take off from a certified airfield. Two books about kayak tours, Randel Washburne's *Kayak Trips in Puget Sound and the San Juan Islands* and *The Maine Island Trail Guidebook* by the Maine Island Trail Association, devote as much space to keeping you out of trouble—both on and off the water—as to describing paddling routes.

While the rule books and bureaucracy associated with organized areas may nettle some of us, the benefits are real. The rules are spelled out and everybody has to play by them. Ironically, such areas of high use are invariably more tidy than remote areas where visitors, though fewer in number, are either unregulated or untutored in the low-impact camping ethic. In organized areas, if we get into trouble, there is usually enough traffic and/or infrastructure for rescue and evacuation. Amenities such as toilets, fire pits, wells, and cleared sites take much of the anxiety out of our planning.

The other characteristic of organized areas is that they are likely to be more crowded than wilderness areas. This requires almost fanatical adherence to the Golden Rule of camping: Leave campsites as neat and clean as you would like to find them. In high-use areas, make sure you use spaces for tents and fires that have already been used or delimited. Cutting out spaces or trampling fragile vegetation to suit your fancy is generally frowned upon, and usually not permitted. That said, you should certainly try to select the best site available. In hot, fair weather you may wish to be on an exposed bluff, point, or beach. In wet, blustery weather, choose a site that is well away from the beach, or back in the trees if such sites are available. "Camp high" is age-old and worthwhile advice, especially if you remember that water flows downhill. Here's another thought: As appealing as a water view might be, the closer to the water you camp, the more likely you are to find yourself immersed in fog that rises off the water after dark or in the morning hours. Sometimes, campsites are too close to the outhouse for my liking; keep looking.

Finally, shop early. Finding your campsite in an organized area isn't the same kind of challenge as locating one on a remote coastline; rather, you may be competing with other campers, and early arrivals are likely to secure the best sites. And don't take any area for granted. Just because an area is organized doesn't mean that the waters and the campsites aren't subject to laws of nature. You need to be just as conscious of location in relation to wind and weather and surf conditions as you would for remote areas. A suitable launching and landing area is a reasonable expectation for a designated site, but don't bet your boat on it. Yes, follow the rules and console yourself with the knowledge that you may not be the discoverer of the lands you visit, but some organization, agency, or volunteer army has made an outdoor camping experience possible where commercial or residential development might otherwise have occurred.

## WILDERNESS SITES

With caveats on the use of this term already expressed, wilderness here designates those areas that do not come under some nicely regulated administrative jurisdiction. In fact, no area is totally without regulation. For example, the possession and/or use of firearms is regulated no matter where you travel, so we may now have the ironic situation of guns being more common in the cities than in the backcountry. This imbalance notwithstanding, I do not carry firearms and do not believe that they are either necessary or desirable, no matter where I might travel. The day when one could plunge into the backcountry and live off the land, hunting game for food, or cutting live trees to create shelter or bedding, is gone. The library is filled with books on survival techniques for the wilderness, and you might find them fun to read; but the reality is that the likelihood of finding yourself in a survival situation is remote.

Finding a campsite in a wilderness setting involves a number of considerations—most of which are also applicable to organized areas, except that in the case of the latter the information may be readily available. In the wilderness setting you may have to do extensive pretrip research or make good guesstimates from your reading of charts and maps, or be forced to evaluate the necessary attributes on the fly. In order of importance, here is a list of attributes to look for:

1. All-weather launching and landing?
2. Space available (tent sites), and nature?
3. All-weather sites?
4. How far from your present site? Is there a backup?
5. Fresh water (not necessary if you carry or fill your tanks en route)?
6. Fires permitted and wood available?
7. Toilet facilities?
8. If site is occupied, can you share (related to 2 and 4, above)?

On rivers and lakes, determining favorable launching and landing sites is not so difficult. But on large bodies of water or in the coastal environment, your assessment of the site is critical. A quiet cove with a gently sloping sandy beach, a bench of land well above the high-tide line, and sufficient shrub or forest cover for wind protection would represent the ideal. A cobbled or rocky beach, if tucked deep in a cove or bay away from the effects of wind and waves, will work if other elements are present, or you might choose the sloping sandy beach in a more exposed environment, gambling on good weather and light surf. The camping kayaker with a loaded boat is not usually the best equipped for doing surf landings. If the beautiful crescent beach is your only choice, consider the "sneak route" that may be found under the horns at either end of the crescent where the swell or wave action is minimized.

We might all like to camp on grass or forest duff, and on a level bench six feet above the beach and tide line; if you find that site, go for it. More often, you may have to settle for camping on rock or sand (see the next chapter for tent and sleeping gear). Either way, make sure that your site is above the high-tide line, and don't be

Three acres of beach become a tiny campsite at high tide.

fooled by those giant bleached logs sitting on the beach. Plenty of kayakers have been awakened in the middle of the night to discover that both they and the logs are awash. It is, in fact, not so unusual to find yourself camped right up against an embankment, or on a sandy bench, and have the midnight high tide only a few feet from your tent door. A miss is as good as a mile.

One tricky subject is the amount of "remodeling" you should do on your site. Is this really a wilderness site, or are you in a regulated area where there are specific limitations on cutting or clearing, or on site location itself? In the case of a truly wilderness site (and normally you are limited by your available tools—a small ax or handsaw, for example), you must use common sense. Certainly, clearing out undergrowth from little-used spaces, or removing the odd bush or tree limb, is acceptable, possibly desirable if the next voyager is going to find a comfortable site. One sure rule is to look for dead or hanging limbs that might descend on your shelter in a good breeze and either get these "turkeys" removed or relocate your shelter.

The best rule, whether you are in an organized area, semiwilderness, or true wilderness, is to leave your site in better shape than you found it. In the case of organized areas, that might mean carrying out someone else's discarded pop cans; in wilderness spots it could mean leveling and clearing a tent site.

You might find an area that is level, grassy, and well above the tide line—yet the terrain is wide open and lacking in trees, shrubs, or even tall grasses to shield you from wind, rain, or even sun. Like the exposed beach landing, either you have no other options, or favorable weather conditions make such a site a reasonable gamble. Under ideal conditions, you may have found the perfect spot. The best of all situations—and such campsites are not uncommon—is an area where you may camp on the beach or out in the open, but where there are also sites cut back in the woods to which you can retreat if the weather deteriorates. Such campsites are not just "all-weather" but all-season.

In Chapter 3 we looked at travel distances and time requirements for making and breaking camp. When you take all of that into consideration, your challenge is to determine that a suitable destination site is within your group's paddling time and distance capabilities. And what if you arrive at 3:00 P.M. and a dumping surf makes landing dangerous or impossible? Suppose there's only space for one tent and you're a party of eight? What's the etiquette if you find a party already camped? If, for whatever reason, you are forced to move on, what backup camping possibilities exist?

An adventure may be defined as a result of poor planning, but if there were no uncertainties, you could just as well have stayed home and watched game shows on the tube. Sometimes you don't get it right or are unlucky, and a bivouac of expediency is your lot. It's surprising how creative we become when faced with the unthinkable situation: no reasonable campsite! The fact is, the more camping you do, the farther afield your adventures take you, the more likely you are to find yourself from time to time up the sound without a campsite. My own experience in thousands of miles of canoe and kayak camping should be some consolation. We have never had to sleep in our boats. Campsites have been hewn from seemingly inhospitable terrain. A few times we paddled after dark. Even such measures of expediency as these can be minimized through careful planning and alert senses. If you remember only one thing, it should be this: In areas where campsites may be few and far between, start looking early—like noon. The incontrovertible rule is that the later the hour, the more tired the crew, the pickier they become about a campsite—and that usually leads to problems.

In the saltwater environment, the location and quality of fresh water becomes a major consideration in locating a camp. Like game trails that magically seem to follow the natural contours, slipping over and around obstacles, so too it is a blessing to discover that campsites are more often than not located near freshwater sources, a spring, or a stream. It is not unreasonable to assume that in any area where someone has camped before, water is nearby. And that camper was likely preceded eons ago by a native person, or more recently by hunters or trappers; they needed water too. If the camp was sited by the Park Service, for example, in an organized area, water availability was probably a criterion. That said, I have camped in the Pacific Northwest on some of the rainiest coasts of North America, which do in fact suffer summer droughts that cause the springs to dry up, or shrivel to unappealing puddles. So wherever you cruise, carry containers for gathering water, and when in doubt about supplies at your intended destination for the day, fill them as you travel. Unlike other camp paraphernalia that may weigh you down, there's no such thing as too much fresh water.

Stoves should be considered essential equipment for kayak campers, and in most nonwilderness areas they are the ecologically right way to go. In those areas where campfires are permitted and wood is plentiful, I am a firm believer in campfires, both for cooking and aesthetics (more on this subject in Chapter 7), but even in areas where dead wood is generally in great abundance, you may find it in short supply, or nonexistent, at heavily used sites. As with water, you may need to gather firewood en route, or send out a freighter kayak or two in search of driftwood from uninhabited beaches.

We address the matter of camp hygiene in the next chapter, but the presence or absence of toilet facilities may be a factor in campsite selection. Typically, in a true wilderness setting the world is your toilet—with all the responsibilities that implies.

## CAMPSITE ETIQUETTE

Finally, what if the campsite about which you have been fantasizing for the last two hours, paddling into a stiff head wind, turns out to have four kayaks and three tents ensconced? If other suitable campsites are nearby—perhaps suitable, but lacking the sunset view or hot springs of your coveted first choice—good manners say you move on. In areas where camping pressure is known to be heavy and available sites few and far between, you should ask the present occupants for "permission" to share the area with them, especially if your own tents and kitchen will be close by. You might, in fact, have to share a kitchen. In any case where travel conditions are risky or the next available campsite is obviously beyond a reasonable paddling distance in daylight hours—where, in fact, pressing on to find unoccupied real estate might put you and your crew at risk—you will usually be urged by the present inhabitants to join them. Over the years, I can recall several disappointments along the lines of the first scenario, but have always found a welcome when circumstances forced us to join earlier settlers. And we have made it our practice to welcome those who found us in "their" camp when they arrived. The good news is that your new neighbors are invariably people like you, and they are out there for the same reasons as you. (Not to foment class warfare, but if your favorite area is also regularly accessed by—and accessible to—powerboats beyond the dinghy class, you may find yourself with noisy and undesirable neighbors. It comes down to planning, again. Don't expect to find your Shangri-la on the Fourth of July, camped two miles from the marina.)

# SHELTER

## THE TENT

If you've found the perfect campsite—high, dry, protected from the wind, and with a flat, grassy area for your tent, a fire pit, and potties maintained by the Park Service—you can probably skim through this chapter. Oh yes, and make sure that you've made a pact with the weatherman to keep your camp high and dry! If a few of these elements of perfection are missing (and it's always best to assume that wind and wet weather are due to arrive at midnight), then you need somewhat more elegance of execution than is required when camping in your backyard. In fact, setting up your tent in the backyard, rigging a rain tarp (more on this subject later), and even giving the tent a hosing-down with a garden hose to test for leakage is a worthwhile pretrip exercise. I own a tent whose quality and engineering are nonpareil, but it took half a dozen setups and careful study of the pole and sleeve configuration before I found a painless and efficient sequence. Screw up the

sequence and my tent setup time goes from ten minutes to half an hour. If a storm or darkness is bearing down on you, or the mosquitoes are attacking, that's the difference between security and frustration.

Ease of setup might be one of your tent purchase criteria, and there are tents that quite literally "pop up," but you should really be more concerned about the finished shelter and feel confident that it is weatherproof. A well-made and durable tent is important to kayak campers because our environment is pretty tough on the equipment. Stuffing and unstuffing a tent and its poles in and out of a wet, sandy kayak in a wet, sandy, salty environment puts a lot of stress on seams, fabrics, and lines—and, of course, the poles and the connecting sleeves, as well. In short, buy the best you can afford. Try to save weight elsewhere—the extra clothes, the food, even your sleeping bag—but choose a heavy-duty tent over the gossamer one. This is where we have it all over the landlubbing backpacker.

## Selection

There are good tents on the market that require stakes to erect, but a better choice is the freestanding variety. The flat, grassy site

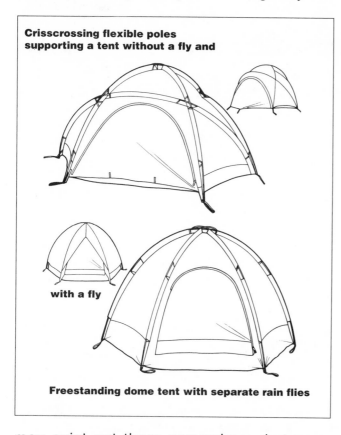

**Crisscrossing flexible poles supporting a tent without a fly and**

**with a fly**

**Freestanding dome tent with separate rain flies**

**A self-supporting A-frame**

and a dome shape are a good idea. Dome tents are characterized by a crisscrossing of three to four long, flexible poles (or wands) arcing through loops or sleeves, and inserted into grommets at each end to create tension and an almost rigid structure.

There are many variations on the "dome" shape, and my own preference is for a somewhat elongated version. Ponder your own claustrophobic tendencies in choosing how tall a tent you really want. The compromise is between weight, windage (how much surface area you present to the weather), and the mole factor. As much as I'd like to be able to stand up, or sit up and wave my arms about, I've decided

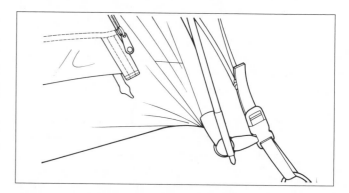

**Some rain flies clip or snap to tent poles.**

may exist out there somewhere, but more likely you'll find yourself on sand, gravel, or two inches of duff on a granite base. Once your freestanding tent is up, stake it down if you can; at least get some gear into it, and/or get it secured to something. A sure thrill is watching your buddies chase their airborne tent down the beach. All else being equal, a taut tent is a dry tent. That's why stakes, additional guylines (from the eaves or sides), that keeping a low profile in camp, as in life, is a good rule to live by. Unless you're camped in the desert, the rain fly should be put over the tent as a matter of course. Some rain flies clip or snap to the poles and/or at the pole ends; some require independent staking. Go for the belt and suspenders. Remember, the tent itself is not rain repellent—often it consists of many panels of mesh—so your fly is your rain protection. Condensation can create more water in the tent than an all-night rain, so good ventilation is important. Examine the zipper and venting options for both fly and tent in your prospective tent, and also be conscious of the need for a uniform separation (creating an air space) between the fly and tent proper.

Finally, you'll see choices of tents with and without vestibules. Get the vestibule. The less stuff there is inside your tent—and that includes clothing bags, your rain gear, your hat, and your sand-covered shoes—the drier and more comfortable you'll be. If you and your gear are forced up against the sides of the tent, that is often sufficient to bring a migration of water to the inside, whether it be condensed moisture or actual rainwater. Also, a ground sheet is an important part of your tent setup. The ground sheet is nothing more than a piece of ten-mil plastic cut *no larger* than the dimensions of the floor of your tent. Although the bottoms of most tents are coated to prevent water from coming up through the bottom, the ground cloth is additional protection, which also forms a barrier between your expensive tent and all the dirty and abrasive elements underneath—pine needles, sand, bottle caps, stones, splinters, and so on.

While we are on the subject of ground, you need to be just as concerned about your foundation and its ability to "perc" as you would be in building a house. We don't dig ditches around tents anymore—or we shouldn't—but a site that

Tent with a space-saving vestibule

slopes away, or is gently rounded, is less likely to let water pool up under your tent. Sand and pea-gravel beaches usually solve the drainage problem, but make sure your "sand" is just that. When it's more mud than sand, you may find yourself on a permanently wet site. The ground cloth can alleviate some of the problem, but pooled water will migrate through all but the heaviest barrier. In fact, choosing your site, setting up your tent, and organizing your bedding (see below) in a manner that limits or guards against pooling water is your best insurance for sleeping dry.

## THE TARP

The tent is where you sleep, but the rain tarp or

A fly tall enough to stand under

fly is where you live. Never leave home without one—maybe two. The fly shields you not only from the rain, but from the sun. If sun is your problem, you'll get little sympathy here. In most coastal environments, you'll be more concerned about staying dry, especially when it's cooking and eating time. We'll call it a rain fly, just to standardize the nomenclature.

Your rain fly can be store-bought—a ten-foot-square coated nylon affair with grommets or loops at each corner and one or two more along each edge—or a roll of sturdy plastic, or poly, similar to the stuff builders use for vapor barriers. You can twist up the corners of this sheeting to affix a line or buy a grommet kit. You can spend more money and buy a fancy parasail-shaped fly, which is lightweight and designed to shed rain and wind more efficiently than a square fly. If you are in a group of four or six persons, you might choose a heavy-duty reinforced nylon or plastic tarp, measuring twelve feet square or larger. Some of these are designed to accommodate a center pole (it

might well be a kayak paddle), and you can create your own "big top."

Since the fly is intended to break the wind and keep the rain off you and the cooking area, you are faced with the challenge of finding anchor points, including the perfectly spaced trees that will coincide with the orientation of campfire or stove relative to the weather. Not infrequently, the spot that best lends itself to rigging a taut fly will determine where everything else goes. In fact, rigging a fly should be the first order of business whenever you land at a new camp.

Anchor points can include trees, bushes, stakes, rocks, overturned kayaks (if you're not going anywhere), or stationary logs and stumps. Your "architecture" is more reliant on having plenty of line than on any grand design. Nylon parachute cord or similar-diameter line is the most suitable construction material. You might also use a heavier cord to create a ridge line. The basic lean-to, with the back end—usually facing the wind—lower than the front, is the design to start with. Hopefully, you will find the

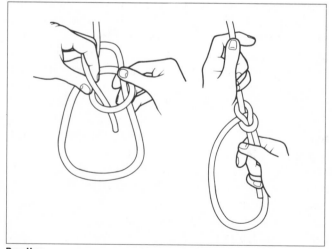

Bowline

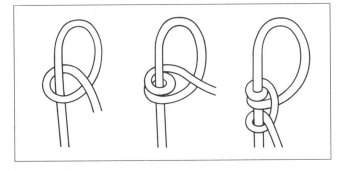

**Taut-line Hitch**

right anchor points, or length of kayak paddle, or forest pole, to get your front corners high enough to accommodate standing guests. That forest pole, however, had better not be from a live tree. Every now and then you'll find a camp where a generation of campers have left such structural aids for the next visitor. You can also carry sectional, or telescoping, aluminum poles just for the fly.

## KNOTS AND LINES

In addition to propitiously spaced anchor points and lots of parachute cord, you'll need a knot. For thirty years, I've gotten by on three knots: square, bowline, and the taut-line hitch. The last of these is the key to a taut tarp. Look at the drawing. The knot's a cinch, literally, and when your fly begins to sag, just tighten the hitch; as the name implies, the more tension, the tighter the line, and the tighter the hitch. That hitch comes in handy when setting up your tent, too. Most new tents have little metal or plastic gizmos that work to tighten the guylines, but they do get lost. Also, there are attachment points on most tents and their rain flies for auxiliary lines when you need to prepare for nasty weather or compensate for an uneven tent site.

Now add a square knot and a bowline to your

repertoire and you're pretty well set. The bowline is for making loops in the end of a line and is the knot of choice for attaching lines to the rain-fly grommets. Either attach the line directly to the bowline loop, or keep a stash of lines of varying lengths, with a bowline loop in the end. Attach a line by simply running the other end of the line through the grommet—or any other attachment point—then back through the bowline loop and pull tight. You've got a bomb-proof attachment, and you can get your line off in just moments when you derig.

You can't carry too much rope, line, or cord. Tightly woven nylon lines or cotton sash cord work well. Clothesline is okay in a pinch, but it tends to swell up with moisture and is not very strong. Carry a variety of diameters. You might consider nylon parachute cord as the standard. This seems to work best for rigging flies and clotheslines (a must in most kayakers' camps); somewhat heavier lines should be on your kayaks for tying up for the night—even if the boats are pulled well up onshore—and heavy-

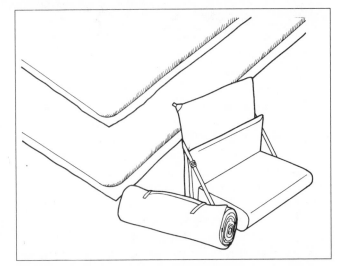

**Therm-a-Rest foam pad and a canvaslike envelope into which you slide the mat to make a chaise longue**

A mummy bag

duty cord should be available for towing boats in an emergency, or creating a reboarding loop in a rescue situation.

## BEDS AND CHAIRS

I've put these two pieces of furniture under one

A rectangular bag

heading because for some years now we've been using a system that some have declared to be the greatest contribution to canoeing and kayaking comfort since the pine bough. The latter, in case you hadn't guessed, is as passé—and as ecologically uncouth—as the ditched tent. One company, Crazy Creek Manufacturing, has popularized a chaise longue that is simply a canvaslike envelope into which you can slide an inflatable mat. The mat is another invention of the recent past called a Therm-a-Rest mattress, a composite of foam and air cells, that self-inflates. It is half the weight and

a fraction of the bulk of the old, tube-style air mattresses that many of us remember, but it gives up very little in comfort. Because of the foam, the foam/air mats are warm; the old tube-style mattresses could be like refrigerator coils on a really cold night. And here is the best part—the foam/air mat is stuffed into the envelope to serve as your mattress at night. Otherwise, it can be converted into a chair or a chaise. Straps and snaps on each side of the envelope create your chair back; the bottom can be left extended like a chaise or doubled back to create a chair and/or lumbar support. As an extra dividend, you end up with a warm chair—a treat when the evening chill begins to descend on camp.

## SLEEPING BAGS

With a foam/air mat underneath, you have already solved one of the problems that even the fullest and puffiest of sleeping bags could not. Whether your bag is stuffed with three pounds of goose down or one of the new synthetic fillers, when you lie down on it, it compresses. Since "loft" and the dead air space that characterizes that puffy bag is what traps and holds your body heat, when you compress the bag under your weight, you've lost your heat. Bottom line: You can get by with a much lighter bag to give you commensurate comfort in any given temperature range if you've got a thermal barrier—like the foam-air combination described above—between you and the ground. The news gets better. Chemists have developed new sleeping-bag fillings that are lighter, loftier, more thermally correct, and less expensive than the down bags we would once have recommended. They are also somewhat hydrophobic—unlike down, which is rendered totally useless if it becomes wet or damp. The fillings carry names like Hollofil, Polarguard, Micro-Loft, and Quallofil.

Everyone has a different personal thermostat; some of us sleep hotter, or colder, than others. But for summer camping most people can choose a bag rated at twenty or forty degrees Fahrenheit. To give you just a starting point, one manufacturer offers a mummy-shaped bag using a proprietary filling (Quallofil, a Du Pont fiber) that is rated at 20 degrees, weighs only three pounds, nine ounces in its stuff bag, and cost under a hundred dollars in 1994. In its stuff bag it measures only nine inches by eight inches, making it easy to stuff into even the stingiest kayak hatch. Scale up from there if you are one who sleeps cold or if you expect to be spending more time in the frigid latitudes.

You have a few other decisions to make.

## LIGHTING OPTIONS

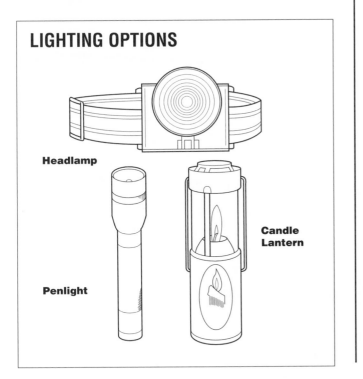

**Headlamp**

**Penlight**

**Candle Lantern**

Rectangular bags provide more room for rollers and twisters than mummy bags, but you have to pack more bulk to get the same temperature rating. If you choose a mummy bag, or if your rectangular bag has a top and bottom, you'll also have to choose a right- or left-hand zipper. Camping couples may find themselves weighing all sorts of possibilities—and compromises—but there are more options for customizing your bedding than you might find for your bedroom at home.

Of course, you can also use that fine down sleeping bag that's been in your closet since backpacking days. Put a thermal mat under it and solve an age-old problem. Just be sure you get the bag into (1) a stuff sack to compress it to a small size, and (2) a second waterproof bag so that it can float at sea for a week without taking water. No kidding! Double-bag your miracle-fiber bag, too. You can put up with a lot of discomfort, including long hours behind the paddle, wind, rain, and camp chores, as long as you know you've got a warm, dry bag to climb into at night. Keeping your bag dry in transit, stuffed into your cockpit or hatch, is an obvious checkpoint. But don't drop your guard just because you got it into the tent. Make sure your bag is on top of the mat, not drooping into puddles that may form on the tent floor. Then, when you go off hiking for the day, make sure the bag is up on the mat and away from the sides of the tent. You might even stuff it back into its bag. When you do have a chance to hang it out, do so, preferably on a clothesline where it can air in the sun. A clean bag, which lofts nicely, is a warm bag.

Some folks value a pillow. There are some inflatable ones, and you can get pillows that double as water carriers. Put a cover over the bladder from a box of wine—I'd suggest drinking the wine first—and you've got a water carrier/pillow for better than free. Or do as I do: My clothes go into my sleeping bag stuff sack. It gets the clothes out of the way, keeps the stuff sack in play, and I don't have to worry about yet another piece of gear.

## OTHER USEFUL GEAR

A ukulele is useful if you enjoy your own music, have room to spare, and are willing to make provision for packing and protecting it. Boxes that make music or noise, like a radio, are not useful and have no place in the kayak camping experience—period! A weather radio for safety reasons (see Chapter 8) is an exception. We'll be dealing separately with kitchens and hygiene, but in the shelter department there really is no other useful gear other than a light source. Even light sources, such as candles, lanterns, and flashlights, are not a real necessity for campers who camp in the summer months. There's usually enough light in the temperate zones, and certainly in the higher latitudes, to illuminate your activities right up until bedtime, and beyond. At a minimum, a penlight is useful for finding the special item buried in your clothing or toiletries pack after you've crawled into the tent for the night. More light than that is desirable if you like to read after dark.

Which suggests another useful item: a book, or books. One could make a case for including a good book under safety equipment. There are times when breaking camp and getting on the water in stormy or unsettled conditions is a very bad idea. Staying in camp and reading is a good way to pass time until conditions improve. Come to think of it, books are a very important—and heavy—part of our camping outfit. Of course, there are guidebooks, sailing directions, chart books, tide and current tables, and local history

(many of the foregoing can be reduced to facsimile or copies), as well as guides to the fauna, flora, and pelagic environment, but much of the weight is just good recreational reading.

If reading light is a must, you can still get by with just a bit more than a penlight. We carry a couple of cigar-sized flashlights, with a twisting head that provides either a focused beam for distance (not particularly useful), or a wide-angle beam for reading. Usually, such a light has a small lanyard that can be used to suspend the light from your tent ridge line or ceiling. These are compact and lightweight enough that each person can carry his or her own.

There are also candle lanterns, propane, and multifuel (including gasoline) light sources. All of these represent a hazard inside a tent, and I do not recommend them. However, used with

A Sun Shower

46

Biodegradable suds can be used with salt water for dishes, hair, and bathing.

light than you might imagine, they are compact, and the fuel and wick can go swimming and still work. The guts of a candle lantern is inert, so it can sit in your camping closet for ten years, or in the bottom of a damp gear pack for a week, and come out ready to use without complaint. And you can bet that it's about as cheap an energy source as you'll find, and won't be offensive to your camping neighbors if they like to turn in early.

As for all those other "useful" items, they're probably not.

## LOCAL MATERIALS

This is a tricky subject. Many beaches and camping areas, especially remote ocean beaches, have a cornucopia of construction materials ranging from the odd stump to plywood and dimensional lumber. Certainly, we can all find comfort in the well-positioned, sculptured log that serves as a seat or backrest, or the stump whose smooth top becomes our kitchen table. As mentioned above, the fortuitous arrangement of such natural flotsam may also serve as the *temporary* anchor point for tents and tarps. Other logs, even logjams, serve as windbreaks, or marinas where we stash our boats for the night; a flat board found on the beach is placed across two logs to form a kitchen shelf. And so on.

But sometimes, the nesting urge can lead to the construction of much more elaborate furniture and/or shelter. Unlike sand castles, which will disappear at high tide, it is possible for such beach architecture to become visual pollution to the traveler who is out there to enjoy the natural world. This is subjective, of course. Finding a kitchen area where the components for comfortable cooking and dining are in place or at hand is often a treat. Com-

care, including plenty of ventilation, they can light up a tent like downtown. They also create an incredible amount of heat in the confines of a tent, which is nice if you are camping in sub-freezing temperatures, not the usual environment for kayak campers. If you have a group larger than two persons and plan to do some cooking after dark, then a small lantern for use in your kitchen area could be useful. The propane lamps are the lightest in weight and easiest to use. Keeping the glass globe and those fragile little mantles from disintegrating in a rough-and-tumble environment, especially when packing and unpacking, is enough discouragement. If you are going to a base camp to hang out for the duration, it's probably okay. The big gasoline, two-mantled lanterns are fine for the KOA, but are not appropriate for the kayak camper's environment. Lighting power of that magnitude can be classified as "visual pollution."

If you must have a lantern, consider carrying the little candle lanterns. They give off more ing upon a beach to find an overly elaborate construction, or the worst—a lean-to with the remains of blue or orange tarp flapping in the wind—is definitely a downer. Deciding what looks "natural" and what does not requires more of a philosopher than I am willing to be, but the same Golden Rule of camping always applies: Leave any camping area looking the way you would like to find it.

## HYGIENE

Here we are talking about keeping clean and taking care of bodily functions. The saltwater environment poses an additional problem: Often you feel uncomfortable, even if you are not dirty. Americans, in general, are overly concerned about cleanliness, taking more baths and showers, and applying more harmful soaps and goos to their bodies than any society in the history of mankind. Such overindulgence has little to do with hygiene. Nobody in our lifetime ever got sick from not taking enough showers!

That said, washing up, taking a shower, shaving, or washing the hair can certainly make you feel more comfortable, even luxurious—especially if you just spent the day at an elevated heart rate with every ninth wave washing over the deck into your face. Your hair, arms, hands, and neck have a quarter inch of rime caked on. You've worked up a good sweat under your parka, polypro, and PFD. That's why somebody invented the Sun Shower, a heavy-duty plastic bag that can hold up to three gallons of water and has a hose and nozzle at one end. You can make your own solar shower using the Mylar liner out of a wine box, replacing the outlet with a hose and nozzle, or you can purchase a commercial model. These usually have a coating designed to absorb sunlight. Even on a cool but sunny day, or on the back deck of your kayak on a hazy day, enough solar energy is absorbed to actually produce hot water. If you can only gather enough rays to produce a tepid shower, even that can be satisfying. The solar shower can be filled with fresh water if you have a ready supply, or salt water. Bathing in salt water, whether ocean-cold or out of a shower, demands that you towel off quickly to prevent the evaporation that will leave an itchy residue.

This leads us to a tricky area. What about soaps and so-called gray water? Saltwater soaps and shampoos can be bought in any outdoors store, and they work. Some call themselves biodegradable, but you should check the label to satisfy yourself. The merits or lack of toxicity of such soaps notwithstanding, on many of the regulated, permit rivers there is a prohibition on using any soap or dumping gray water into the river; the usual procedure calls for digging and lining a small drain field well away from the river. This would certainly be a desirable approach for coastal campers, but except for the most heavily used beach camping areas, most beaches are themselves natural drain fields, and if your shower or shaving water falls on the beach below the high-tide line, the tremendous volume and flushing action of sea water makes the practice acceptable. The rules change on rock and earthen surfaces, and with larger parties (which we would discourage in any event). The drain field in the woods is de rigueur for these situations. Sanitary or polluting considerations aside, the amount and disposal of suds is a Golden Rule matter. If it's noticeable to your neighbors or the next campers, you've broken the rule. More on the subject when we come to the kitchen.

Gray water's a cinch compared with the problem of human waste or excrement. As more and more folks take to the trails, on land and water, this has become a monumental problem. The regulated rivers mentioned above have elaborate requirements for the handling of human waste;—not just carrying out, but disposing of it at trip's end. For coastal kayakers in organized areas there are usually pit toilets maintained by park or other public personnel. But, beyond the organized areas, the matter is one of concern. How serious is the problem? Enough so that an environmentally concerned woman by the name of Kathleen Meyer wrote a book a few years ago entitled *How to Shit in the Woods*. This book was a best-seller and continues to be required reading for anyone who plans to spend time in the backcountry. Although the book was written before the explosion in sea kayaking, and the consequent increased pressures on our already beleaguered shorelines, its message and specific techniques are applicable to the coastal paddler.

I am not aware at this time of any coastal areas where carrying out human waste is required, as is the case for permit rivers, but don't be surprised to see it happen. You might wish to adopt a plan for yourself, in any event. There are a number of commercial products on the market that address the problem, and these may, in fact, be a boon to a new breed of camper who is perhaps more fastidious than some of us who grew up in an earlier era. On the river, a popular arrangement has been the ubiquitous ammo can, lined with a plastic bag and often topped with a real toilet seat. A bit of lye and a scoop is the parting gesture. The toilet paper, which also poses a problem, goes into a separate container for either burning or later disposal.

Fortunately, areas of high coastal traffic, usually more accessible to maintenance people than canyon-bound rivers, get their pit toilets when the pressures become too intense. Otherwise, you have two choices: the woods or the beach—well below high-tide line in the latter case. This is acceptable in the most remote and lightly traveled areas, but can pose serious problems as you get closer to civilization and increased traffic. The solid waste may disperse, but the toilet paper should be burned. The "woods" is not such a straightforward proposition as it might seem. The first necessity is for disposal, not only well away from camp—at least one hundred yards—but away from trails. Digging a hole and burying deep is the recommended practice, but consider water sources, drainage patterns, and the like. Also, there may be areas where disposal out in the open may be preferable to burying, if the latter tends to preserve, rather than hasten decomposition. Meyer's book is quite instructive on all of the possibilities.

We can't write a treatise—or improve upon Meyer's work—here, but the important thing is to have a plan and an ethic. Start by making sure that either your party carries the necessary digging implement—a sturdy folding shovel, preferably—or each member carries a personal trowel.

As with many matters of camping etiquette, common sense should rule. Consider your own disgust when you come upon human waste and/or bushes festooned with toilet paper. Depending on your area and the nature of human traffic, have the tools and the plan for ensuring that no other camper is put at visual or hygienic risk by your imprudent actions.

# KITCHEN AND CUPBOARD

Eating well may be a major focus of the kayak camper. Unless you are in the expedition mode, meal preparation and the enjoyment of a menu as varied and sumptuous as you might have at home is a reasonable, even admirable, goal. This chapter should convince you there's no limit to the culinary possibilities. With the carrying capacity of our boats, the cooking equipment and accessories available, and the combined variety of whole and packaged foods, we can be floating gourmets. To put a little different spin on the homily about eating to live: You can eat to paddle or paddle to eat—or both.

## WHERE

The location of your kitchen may be determined for you by the nature of the campsite. Many organized areas have picnic tables and/or fire grates, normally off the beach. Making a kitchen area on the beach may be desirable where logs and other flotsam create natural kitchen counters and stovetops, and tables and chairs as well. In areas where driftwood is plentiful, you may find that cooking fuel is to be had for the reaching. Cooking fires are suggested only under the following conditions: They are permitted to begin with; they are kept small and built on a spot where previous campers have cooked; if they can't be built on sand or gravel that will be scoured by the tides, consider using a fire pan; don't allow the fire to char the drift logs, which may otherwise serve as handy windbreaks. If you are not handy with a cooking fire to begin with, forget about it altogether and use cook stoves.

Beach kitchens have the advantage, other than aesthetic pleasure, of being near the water for washing and rinsing, and keeping good space between food and tents. Also, since kayak hatches are the best place to store food for the night, your kitchen and cupboards are in close proximity. Another consideration in choosing or rejecting the beach for your kitchen is weather. In cold, wet, or windy weather the woods may be more inviting, and you need to figure out where you can best rig a rain fly for cooking and/or dining comfort. The absence of trees and good anchoring points may decide the matter for you.

Up in the woods, the protocol is no different from that which canoe campers and backpackers might observe. Conditions for building fires are really no different from on the beach, except now you must be conscious of the fire hazards that may be associated with surrounding grasses, woods, or even underground roots. Usually, a cook stove is the preferred alternative.

## FIRES AND GRATES

In certain organized areas you may find what might be called "Park Service Grates." These are throwbacks to a misguided past. They are enormous cement and iron things that invite the use of big logs and conflagrations that are more bonfire than cooking fire. If you must have a fire, do yourself and the world a favor: Throw back the grate and build a little kitchen fire down inside the fortress using the cement sides as your windbreak. A little backpacker's grate set on two flat rocks (about four inches high) is more than sufficient. Here's another suggestion: Don't buy a cooking grate with legs; or, buy one and cut the legs off. For thirty years, we have carried a tiny metal grate such as the one shown in the picture; it's only fourteen inches long, five inches wide at the wide end, and weighs ounces. We have cooked meals for six on it.

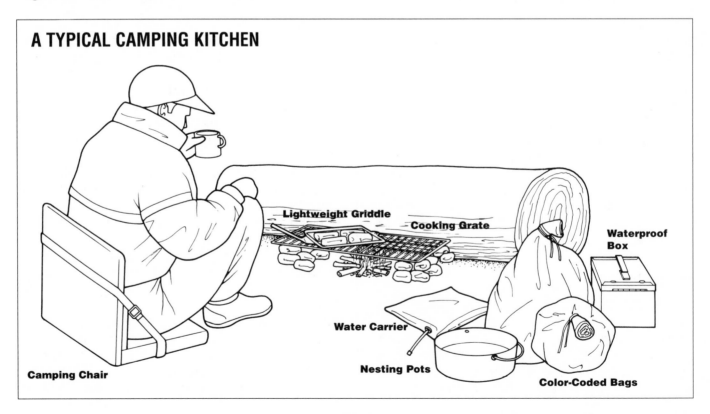

## A TYPICAL CAMPING KITCHEN

Lightweight Griddle

Cooking Grate

Waterproof Box

Water Carrier

Camping Chair

Nesting Pots

Color-Coded Bags

# STOVES

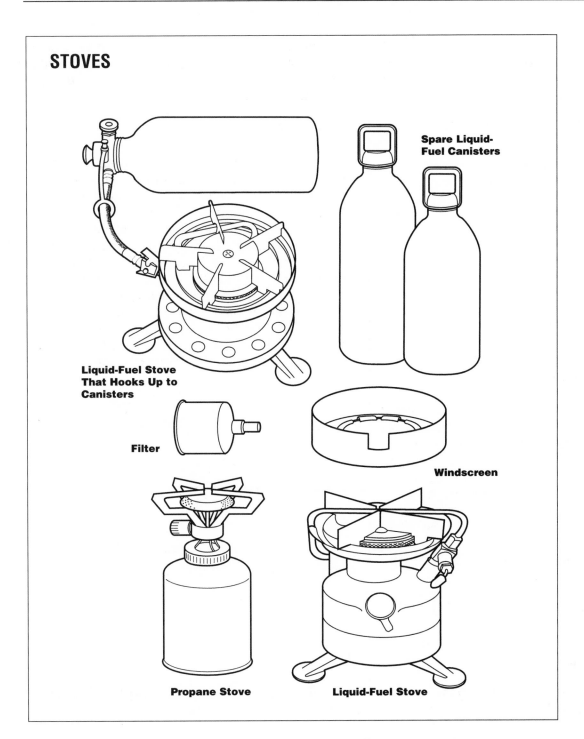

Spare Liquid-
Fuel Canisters

Liquid-Fuel Stove
That Hooks Up to
Canisters

Filter

Windscreen

Propane Stove

Liquid-Fuel Stove

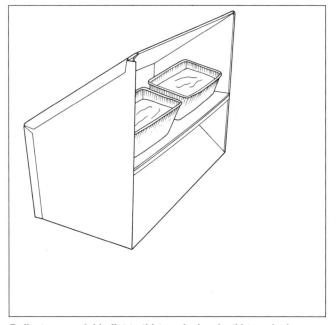

Reflector oven folds flat to thirteen inches by thirteen inches and weighs less than two pounds.

So much for fires. I don't want to encourage their use, but if they are permitted and wood is plentiful, they are a reasonable option. Just remember, small is beautiful. You shouldn't need a saw or an ax; what you need can be broken by hand or with a rock, and longer pieces can be simply fed into the fire. If you want to carry the bulk, and there may be a meal or two where you want to splurge, you can carry charcoal. Have a barbecue or use briquettes with a Dutch oven (see below).

There are no instructions here on starting a fire in the rain because if you aren't a pro in the construction and care of cooking fires, maybe you should go the stove route. When we get to the section on foods below, you may see why stoves are the way to go, in any event; you'll have greater control and you'll literally feel more at home. Our own practice is to use a combina-

tion of stove and a small fire. The latter is used mainly to keep the coffee hot and to heat water (usually sea water) for doing the dishes and burning paper and packaging.

## STOVES

A visit to any backpacker's or outdoor equipment store will introduce you to a wide variety of cooking apparatus. We've actually carried and used a Coleman two-burner gas stove. It's a luxurious appliance but not recommended because even if you've got a big double kayak with hatches that will accommodate it, a lot of cubic volume is taken up by the metal box itself. If you want or need two burners, you will have more flexibility, both for your cooking and for packing the boat, if you choose two single-burner stoves. Despite the variety of stove models, your essential decision concerns the

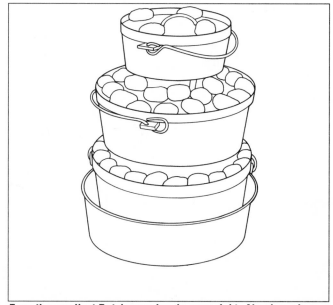

Even the smallest Dutch oven is a heavyweight. Aluminum is a better choice than cast iron for kayakers.

## OUTBACK OVEN

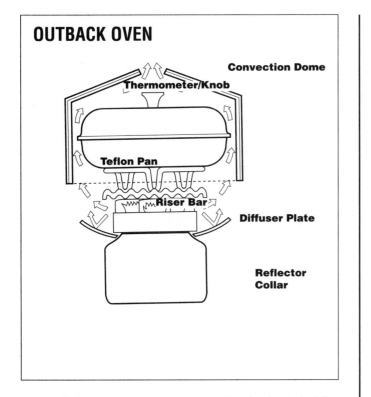

Convection Dome
Thermometer/Knob
Teflon Pan
Riser Bar
Diffuser Plate
Reflector Collar

type of fuel: propane gas or liquid fuel (white stove fuel or unleaded gasoline). Propane stoves are the simplest to maintain and operate, and they are inexpensive. They are quiet, burn cleanly, and adjusting the flame seems more precise than with liquid-fuel stoves. There is no gasoline smell or spillage to worry about. Their downside is that propane tanks to fit your particular unit may not be available except at specialty outdoor stores; you'll have to maintain your own inventory. Also, the spent canisters, which cannot be crushed, must be carried home and disposed of.

The advantage of liquid-fuel stoves, especially those that burn multi-fuels or unleaded gasoline, is that you can always find fuel, even in the most remote or primitive locations. Gasoline stoves also tend to have a higher high-heat range than propane. Your gasoline is normally carried in canisters like those pictured on page 53, and they are, of course, refillable. Mechanically, the liquid-fuel stoves are considerably more complicated than their propane counterparts; there are pumps and valves, and eventually the gaskets wear out or the valves clog. Carrying spares is a good idea if your stove has a lot of mileage on it, or if you are going to be on an extended journey. And for long trips, the liquid-fuel stove makes sense if you don't want to be hauling around a boatful of new and empty propane canisters. Carry a small funnel for filling your stove. Use canisters with a totally secure screw-top. A spill or leakage in your hatch with the sleeping bag and pile sweater can be an expensive annoyance.

Our choice? We have one of each!

## OVENS

Every stove needs an oven. An old standby is a reflector oven used with an open fire. It is an aluminum folding contraption with top, bottom, sides, and a baking shelf. You face the opening toward your fire and place your breads, muffins, pizzas, or whatever on the shelf. Keeping a hot fire close to the mouth of your oven—but not too close—is a challenge, but the results can be gratifying. The reflector oven weighs two pounds and folds flat to a thirteen-by-thirteen-inch package. It's inexpensive, lightweight, compact, and versatile, but it requires good fire maintenance skills, abetted by a dependable supply of nice firewood.

Another choice—believe it or not—is a Dutch oven. This is for the floating gourmet who is willing to carry the weight and the bulk. There is an entire literature of Dutch-oven cooking and baking in the outdoors, an art revived largely by the river rafters. The rafters, if one is to make a judgment based solely on the cornu-copia of gear they can haul in their inflatable monsters, are truly masters of itinerant gastron-omy. Fire is of course a Dutch-oven requisite, and although you can create your own char-coal, it is just as well to carry briquettes. Only a few are necessary, placed on the lid of the oven to create the even heat that makes the Dutch oven such a great cook's tool. You can save a good deal of weight and sacrifice only a bit of that prized evenness of heat by choosing cast aluminum rather than the traditional cast-iron stove. My wife and I still carry and use a Dutch oven, especially for family-style trips where eating is more important than paddling, but there are some other options that don't re-quire an open fire, weigh considerably less, and take up less space.

A simple device is the Bakepacker, a six- to seven-inch-diameter ring with a grating of baf-fles designed to disperse heat inside a four-quart cookpot. The Bakepacker is placed in the pot with just enough water covering the bottom to create steam heat. You are not steaming your muffins, cake, or bread, though; these are placed inside a plastic bag—actually a bake bag—which sits on the Bakepacker grate. Sim-ple, yes, but somewhat limited. For those who really want to bake and dine in style, the most ingenious cooking apparatus we've found is called the Outback Oven. This neat invention is compact and weighs only a pound and a half. Consisting of a Teflon pan—which can also be used as a fry pan—a reflector collar, diffuser plate, cover, and soft convection dome, the oven is placed on a conventional propane stove. A thermometer in the cover gives almost foolproof readings to produce cakes, pies, muffins, breads, or quiches—in fact, almost anything you would bake in your home oven. As much as we love the Dutch oven and its

nostalgic overtones, the Outback Oven is a much more sensible option. A whole line of mixes have been created for both the Bakepacker and Outback Oven; they are good, but we have found equal success with the stan-dard packaged mixes right from the supermar-ket. You are also free to bake from scratch, but you'd be wise to premix the dry ingredients in your kitchen and carry them in zipper-style bags with the written instructions stuck into the package.

## OTHER KITCHEN HARDWARE

There are various stove accessories, such as windscreens, stands, and fuel filters, but the only essential one is a match or the equivalent. You may also choose battery-powered "matches," which produce a spark with the pull of a trigger, or carry the simple propane cigarette lighters that sell for less than a buck in almost any convenience store. If your "stove" is going to be a fire, take waterproof matches. There are ones with long-lasting flames, as well as fire sticks that combine flame and tin-der in one. A candle is a time-honored fire starter for your darkest, wettest moments.

Now that you've got your stove and oven, there is all that other hardware to consider: pots, pans, utensils, pot grabbers, spatulas, la-dles—in fact, whatever you might find in your own kitchen drawers at home. The problem be-comes one of what not to take, since there is certainly no limit to what you might find useful. For example, a whisk might come in handy, but can you achieve your objective with a fork? Like many other decisions with respect to your camping gear, you must literally weigh the con-venience or utility value against time and space constraints. The two-person expedition, need-ing to make long mileage each day, will want a simple outfit that is light in weight, quick to set up, take down, and use on the fly. A larger group that intends to make itself comfortable in a base camp, where eating is a focal point of the adventure, is going to make room for a full range of cooking paraphernalia.

Let's consider coffee. Our expeditioners may be happy with powdered crystals that can produce a cup of java in minutes, using the same pot of boiling water that will be used to make the instant oatmeal. The floating gourmets, however, will carry a custom-ground roast, plastic funnel, and paper filters, and will brew the coffee straight into a thermos jug to keep it hot. Or there's cowboy coffee, which is great for a large group of back-to-basics expeditioners: Just put a handful—that's maybe ten tablespoons for the fastidious cowboy—of percolator-grind coffee into a two-quart pot of water. Put a lid on the pot and bring it to an explosive boil. The moment your pot "burps," usually knocking the lid off with an eruption of grounds, get the pot off the fire and pour half a cup of cold water into it. That settles the grounds, and you can then ladle out your coffee. Your last two cups of coffee are like high-octane espresso, and you'll be left with an undrinkable sludge at the bottom of the pot. I've made lots of cowboy coffee over the years and it's as good as the Yuppie stuff, but where fresh water is at a premium, it's a water waster.

And so it goes. Do you want fresh-baked muffins or will you be just as happy with bagels from the supermarket, or, for the truly trail-hardened, pilot biscuits. Regardless of how simple or elaborate your menu, there may be some minimal components for a cooking outfit.

Start with the cook kit. One large pot, say four quarts, can serve many functions, beginning with the fact that you can pack stuff in it. It's a water carrier, a sink, and a cooking vessel. If your meals tend to be of the one-pot variety, then all the water you need gets boiled at once and distributed to its other uses. The final use may be for rinsing dishes, or even as shaving water. A smaller pot—two-quart size or less—can be used for mixing or cooking. A frying pan may also double as a lid for the large pot.

Regardless of your pot-and-pan combination, disdain the flimsy little handles or pot grabbers that are offered with various kits and use a pair of gooseneck pliers. You'll have not only a substantial tool for repair purposes, but something that can be used to lift four boiling quarts of water off a flaming wood fire, no matter where the little handle receptacle is. You can dispense with the whisk, but don't leave home without a spatula. A wooden spoon is nice for serving up hot cereal and other one-pot dishes. A hot mitt is especially useful if you are using a cooking fire.

Plastic cups don't cook your hands and will keep hot fluids warmer longer than metal. Likewise, you can replace the metal plates in your kit with plastic bowls. They keep the food warmer and your hot meal can't slide off into the sand so easily. Don't forget to carry a can opener; it's hard to outfit a camp kitchen without some canned items, it seems. It's hardly indispensable, but we often carry a griddle, especially if a cooking fire is going to be used. They usually weigh less than a frying pan but provide two to three times as much cooking area, and they rest nicely on a rectangular fire grate.

Although not properly a utensil or hardware, some sort of box, wanigan, or other hard-shelled container makes for a tidier kitchen. There are some things that just don't seem to belong in a bag or soft pack. Boxes and kayak hulls don't mix very well, but you might find a plastic or Tupperware-type container in which you keep such items as spices, the matches, items for lunch, food leftovers, or any crush-ables. One of the best organizers for kitchen paraphernalia is a large, zippered pouch made of a heavy-gauge, water-resistant fabric and containing mesh inner bags for your utensils. Elastic loops hold up to a dozen small contain-ers (like 35 mm film canisters) for spices or cooking oil. This may be where your dish soap and a small sponge reside as well.

# GOING TO MARKET

## Menu Planning

Paddlers travel on their stomachs. Unless you are on an expedition requiring frequent making and breaking of camp, or your itinerary calls for long hours of paddling, thus limiting the amount of time you can devote to meal preparation, think about the kinds of meals you like to have at home, or at a restaurant. Your "backpack on the water," as you'll recall from Chapter 1, is not so cramped as the terrestrial variety, so you can afford to carry food in quantity and quality. If you are planning to be out for a long weekend, or less than a week, consider carrying mostly whole foods from the supermarket. They can include fresh meats, fresh whole vegetables and potatoes, rice, or pastas. Some canned goods are okay, but you have to carry the water that they are packed in. You can carry real eggs in their shells (pack them in a plastic con-tainer padded with paper towels), or put half a dozen shelled eggs into a screw-top container.

Our other breakfast staples include coffee, powdered juices, hot cereals, granola, bacon, and pancake mix. Unless you are going to be baking fresh, you'll rely on hard bread and rolls for the first several days; the kayaker's staff of life is the bagel. It's compact and can withstand a fair amount of abuse; plus, a pack of six or eight bagels is shaped about right for stuffing into a kayak hull. After a couple of days, you will probably have to switch to really hard breads—call them crackers if you will—like Wasa bread or Ry-Krisp. Earlier I mentioned pilot biscuits disparagingly, but they are, in fact, quite palatable and durable indeed. They are flat hard biscuits that taste like day-old pizza crust, and when you goop them up with plenty of peanut butter and honey, or layer on some fine hard cheese and salami, you might even develop a liking for them. We have actually car-ried over pilot biscuits from one paddling sea-son to the next—and they still taste like day-old pizza crust.

Already I've described some staple items for breakfast and lunch. An organizational ploy you might consider is to buy and pack breakfast and dinner foods for all members of the group—presumably after some democratic so-licitation of wishes, wants, and no-goes—but have each person provide his or her own lunches and or snacks. It's one meal you don't have to worry about, and everyone can indulge personal tastes. Some people seem happy munching a few cookies or gorp washed down with Gatorade; others will require more elabo-rate provisions. If you don't know "gorp," it's a concoction of nuts, seeds, M&M's, and dried fruits, in whatever portions you prefer, and usu-ally available in larger supermarkets in dis-pensers from which you can mix and match your custom blend. One concession to togeth-erness at lunch might be a boiling pot of water for those who want coffee, tea, or soup from a dried mix or bouillon cubes.

Breakfasts and lunches can be very simple affairs. The most complicated breakfast might be pancakes, but they are a great treat for the morning when you have extra time. What makes them complicated is the inability, even with a large griddle, to make them in quantity quickly enough. Honey is a more efficient and compact topping than syrup, but if you crave the latter, consider adding a bit of water to a cup of brown sugar and bringing it to a simmering boil. Your brown sugar can do double duty as an all-purpose sweetener and as syrup.

Another item that seems to pose a challenge for campers is milk. Even if you and the kids can forgo your daily glass of milk, there seem to be recipes, hot cereals, and cups of coffee that cry out for milk. As for the daily

**Going Shopping**

Food won't be your only supermarket purchase. Here are a few of the other kitchen items you will find there.

For dishwashing:
- paper towels
- sponge
- plastic scrubber

For packing:
- freezer bags for repackaging food
- garbage bags for repackaging and packing out
- plastic snap-top containers
- an indelible marker for identifying what's in your food packs

For cooking:
- matches
- charcoal briquettes

glass, you would do better to train your palate for orange juice crystals and water; otherwise, it's powdered milk. You can make powdered milk almost potable by adding a touch of sugar and aerating the mixture by pouring it back and forth between two pots as you mix. For other milk needs, carry condensed milk in cans; or, you can now find in most supermarkets boxed whole milk that requires no refrigeration.

## KEEPING FOOD FRESH

Dinner poses the true challenge, and it's the time for floating gourmets to let out all the stops. If you will accept the proposition that you can enjoy essentially the same foods you would prepare at home, then it's not appropriate to recommend this or that specific item of meat, potato, pasta, or vegetable. Rather, what is important is the form. Let's take meat, be it chicken, beef, pork, or lamb. The number of days out will dictate a progression from fresh, to canned, to freeze-dried. You might be able to go two nights with fresh meat, keeping it in a soft-sided pack and using the freeze bags—they have some kind of magic blue fluid in them—or our favorite technique: freeze half a dozen cans of beer and use them as your refrigeration system. They'll keep your perishables cold for a full day, or more if the weather's not too hot, and as their value as a refrigerant wanes they become just a nice cool quaff. The cans crush to flat little wafers you can carry out.

On day three, you will probably have to go to canned meats. If you were enjoying bacon with breakfast, you can extend the fresh period by carrying slab, rather than sliced, bacon, and then move to canned bacon or Spam. Finally, as your time out progresses, if meat is still important to your diet or your tastes, you will be forced to use freeze-dried meat, or more likely, packaged dinners including the meat. Freeze-dried meals are very expensive, but they do have some very attractive attributes. There are a tremendous variety and some very creative and tasty dishes, and they are extremely easy to prepare. It's not a bad idea to have a freeze-dried meal or two as emergency or layover rations if your itinerary gets pushed by wind or weather. They are lightweight and packed to last a century, so they are the answer to space and weight constraints on an extended trip.

One tip on carrying and using freeze-dried meals: The portions are often too small to satisfy the fuel requirements of an adult paddling machine, so plan to supplement your freeze-dried entrée with extra rice, potatoes, pastas, or baked breads and biscuits. You can, of course, double the portions, but be warned that the cost per calorie becomes astronomical; you could do better paddling to the nearest bed and breakfast with a four-star kitchen.

Vegetarians and pasta lovers have a better deal. Vegetables stay fresh longer, especially the durable ones like carrots and onions. They can add crunch to an otherwise squishy diet. As with meat, as the trip extends you can move from fresh, to canned, to dried. One luxury for the camper is the crispiness of a salad. A head of cabbage is an incredibly durable item, so carry several. In the early days of the trip they can be cut up and served with a little lemon juice for a simple and tasty salad. Later they can be cooked up as a side dish or as part of a stew. Potatoes can be carried whole; only weight, not durability, may limit the poundage you wish to haul aboard. In addition to potatoes and rice, pastas, Top Ramen, and legumes such as dried lentils or beans are a great source of concentrated carbohydrates and should ideally constitute the major source of fuel for any self-powered endeavor. All of the latter have a high ratio of fuel-to-weight value, with the added attraction of packability and durability. In fact, if fuel rather than palate pleasing were the prime criterion, one could pack nothing but "glue": cereals, wheat and corn flours, starches, pasta, and legumes. You'd run a clean engine, but perhaps expire from dietary boredom.

You can find a fair variety of dried or instant packaged dinners in the supermarket, but at some point you are forced to visit the specialty outdoor retailer. Here you will find freeze-dried foods and meals, specialized matches and fire starters, biodegradable and saltwater soaps, propane tanks, candles to fit the candle lantern, and stove fuel (also available in most hardware stores). Not to begrudge the outdoor stores the business they rightfully earn with their quality and specialized products, but a worthwhile approach to stocking the kayak camping kitchen is to see how much you can assemble from the supermarket before heading to a specialty store.

## PACKING

Here's the real challenge. There are three main objectives: reducing packaging bulk, that is, getting rid of most of the original packaging materials; creating meal-sized portions; and reducing camp kitchen chaos, as in, "Where the *&%$# are the lentils?"

Let's start with the first and second objectives, which are intertwined. You are going to

Gaffing the catch of the day

get rid of virtually all of the cardboard, glass, cellophane, foam, and plastic packaging materials because you need to distribute bulk items to their meal portions and because the store packaging is too bulky, misshapen, and not waterproof. The best repackaging container is the zippered plastic bag; if you choose light-gauge bags, double them. The freezer bags are sturdy enough that one will suffice, and they are tough enough to be reused. If you are a belt-and-suspenders kind of person, or you are going on an extended expedition, you can increase your insurance by putting groups of repackaged foods into cloth bags. These reduce the puncturability of your food bags and are easy to label with a laundry marker. Whether you go the cloth bag route or just go with single freezer bags, your final meal groups can go into waterproof or dry bags. The most utilitarian and cost-effective ones are semitransparent with a fold-over top and Fastex buckle. They are reasonably inexpensive, are easy to open and close, and come in a variety of sizes, affording flexibility when it comes to finally stuffing them into the kayak. So don't get all large-sized bags; you'll want some that fit into the nooks and crannies, and some that help identify the contents by their size. The freeze-dried meals are generally packaged in watertight and near-indestructible foil/plastic packages, so you can usually just cram these into your final food bags.

While you are doing all this repackaging, you are also trying to figure out a distribution of portions that will reduce the fire drill at mealtime. The bulk and staple items like rice, pasta, hot cereal, pancake mixes, and the like have to be broken down into meals and, to get it right, amalgamated with the other breakfast or dinner components in the final waterproof bags, which will ideally be "Dinners" or "Breakfasts." De-

pending upon your organizational zeal, or perhaps the length of trip or number of persons, some foods, flavorings, condiments, or staples may be left in bulk. If your breakfasts are all oatmeal, pancakes, or granola, you could simply have a breakfast bag containing these in bulk. The problem with this system is that you might overindulge on pancake mix on day one, and find yourself with less than a meal-sized portion by day four. Better to make the portion measurements in the comfort of your kitchen beforehand. When you grab your breakfast bag marked "Day 3" with its premeasured portions for six persons, you know what you're getting and, more important, what you have left. Some staples like sugar, powdered juices, and flour for yet-undesignated use can be left in bulk; just make sure you've packed more than enough, knowing you'll probably be taking some of it home. Here's another tip. If you have repackaged prepared mixes like Bisquick, Minute Rice, Cream of Wheat, or Rice-A-Roni, make sure you cut out the mixing instructions from the package and stick these in the zipper bag with the mix.

## SECURING THE FOOD

In certain parts of the world, bears represent a threat to your kitchen—and possibly to your person, if they go looking for food in your camp and come face-to-face with you. You can find plenty of reading and advice on dealing with bears, so we won't explore the subject deeply here, but if you take the precautions that you must take with some smaller critters, you will have also taken the steps that can keep you out of bear trouble. The biggest threat to your food supply is not, in fact, bears, but squirrels, chipmunks, raccoons, and crows. As in dealing with any thief, you don't want to draw attention to your valuables—in this case, your food. Start by keeping a clean camp and clean kitchen. Don't leave food or garbage around the camp at any time, other than when you are eating and preparing your meals. Even dirty pans or food containers with the smell of food can bring uninvited guests. When you are not in camp, take your food with you, in the hatches of your kayak. Do the same at night. Your kayak hatches are the safest place to stash your foodstuffs. Don't take food into the tent with you. If you leave food bags around camp, unless they are made of chain link, any or all of the above-mentioned critters can find their way into them. A crow can peck a hole in your plastic food bag faster than you can open it. I won't claim that a raccoon can undo a Fastex buckle, but I won't bet against it, either.

## FISHING AND FORAGING

Some folks fish for sport, others fish for food. We've included this topic here for good reason. First, don't plan your meals around the certainty of catching fish or finding a productive bed of clams or oysters. Do plan to do some fishing and gathering, because if you are successful, the bounty of the sea can make any kayak camping trip a special occasion. Over the years we have dined on fresh ling-cod, rock fish, dogfish seviche, sautéed sea urchin roe, sea cucumber, mussels, oysters, and crab. On one trip we spent hours digging for giant geoducks, a sort of a clam on steroids declared by some to be a great delicacy. We were skunked on the geoducks, but for our effort were rewarded with several buckets of succulent butter clams.

The areas where you might paddle and fish or forage are too numerous and varied for us to get specific about types of fish or shellfish and techniques for bringing them home to dinner. There are also many areas where harvesting restrictions may apply to certain species for reasons of preservation, pollution, or—in certain seasons in the Pacific Northwest—danger of PSP (paralytic shellfish poisoning). For your destination, you will need to do some research on species and any local restrictions and/or hazards or prohibitions that might apply. Your best introduction to living off the sea will be to go out with someone who is an accomplished forager, or spend some time with locals who can steer you to the right places with the right stuff.

That said, your minimal outfit can be a hand line and a bunch of "lead heads" with plastic worms, and as you get the foraging bug, grow to rods and reels, salmon-trolling rigs, crab traps, and clam shovels. Let's look at that minimal rig, because the investment is low and the potential returns high. Even though you are hunting for food, there is great sport in hauling fish into a kayak using a simple hand line. It's primitive and exhilarating. The hand line is nothing more than thirty- to sixty-pound test monofilament line wound onto a plastic ring. You can loop a line through the center of the ring on the deck in front of you, leaving your hands free to paddle, so you can troll or move on to the next fishing spot. No matter where you are, weighted lures like the lead-head worm or Buzz Bomb lures available in any tackle store can be used effectively for bottom fish. You want to find a relatively calm area, a drop-off from a reef or point, or on the edge of a kelp bed, where you can let out line until it hits bottom. Reel up your lure a couple of feet off the bottom, and then commence jigging by raising your lure up and down in long, deliberate movements.

When your wish comes true and you hook a

fish—and there is a high probability that you will—your problems are just beginning. How to get five pounds of wriggling, spiny, barracuda-toothed critter into your kayak? You should have several tools close at hand, on deck or in "holsters" on your person: a small folding gaff or a net to get the fish out of the water, a set of heavy pliers for stunning the fish and getting the hook(s) out of its mouth, and a sharp knife. The latter may be used variously for subduing a larger fish, cutting a hook out of the fish, or—if you've hooked something you don't want to deal with, like an oversized dogfish shark or an eighty-pound halibut—cutting him loose and chalking up the loss of your lure to experience.

Whether it's a five-pound cod or that eighty-pound halibut, fishing out of a twenty four-inch-wide kayak does pose certain hazards, especially in the heat of battle. Some boats are more stable than others, making them more suitable for fishing, but if you are less than confident about doing a juggling act with boat, paddle, reels, lines, and an angry fish, there are two remedies. Get a set of spon-sons—inflatable tubes that run alongside your cockpit and give you almost another foot of boat width—and rig a paddle park using two cleats in front of your cockpit and an elastic cord. The paddle sits on the two cleats and you simply stretch the cord over the shaft and the ends of the cleats so you can grab it when you need it.

This is barely an introduction to the subject, but it's well worth your further reading and re-search. The kayak makes a great vehicle for stalking the seas, and unlike the folks out there raking the waters with thousands of dol-lars worth of gear, out of boats costing tens of thousands, you can find priceless rewards with minimal effort and investment. Believe me, hauling a ten-pound lingcod into a skinny kayak is a thrilling experience and just a pre-lude to a dining triumph.

## CLEANING UP THE MESS

Your kitchen and cooking efforts pose the greatest potential ecological and hygienic prob-lems. We have discussed the importance of low-impact fire building, and using fire pans in certain areas, or using stoves exclusively. All food containers, cans, and packaging must be packed out. You can burn up paper, cardboard (most of this should have been disposed of at home in your repackaging operation), plastic wrap, and cellophane if you have a fire, but foil and cans—even if you put them in the fire to burn out the residual food—must be gotten out of the fire and carried out as well. If you have used a fire, make sure you break up any re-maining coals and drown the fire pit and any residual coals with water.

If you have used no open fire—and there are many areas where fires will be neither appro-priate nor permitted—you still have garbage and dishwashing to deal with. Careful planning to minimize the amount of waste food is the first step. Small amounts of food can be rinsed out to sea, but in areas where you are sharing space with other campers, consider the visual pollution caused by dumping half a pot of oat-meal onto the rocks near your beach. Sure, the tides will take it away eventually; in the mean-time, your neighbors are treated to an ugly scene. Burying food in the woods is equally ob-noxious, because eventually some animal is going to dig up the whole mess. If you are going to clean fish, do it well away from your camp, or your neighbor's camp. Fish heads and entrails seem to pose less of a problem than a pot of oatmeal. Usually, by the time you've cleaned the last fish, the ravens and gulls will have carried off everything but the fish scales. I was cleaning a few small bass on the rocks near camp in the Gulf Islands off the coast of British Columbia one time, and as I turned my back on the pile of hard-won fillets to talk to a friend, a dive-bombing raven carried away one of my prizes. Later, we witnessed an eagle and a crow in a tug-of-war and screaming match over one of the fish heads.

The beach sand and gravel are a natural drain field, so a certain amount of scouring and rinsing can take place on the shore. While you wade a few feet out in your gum boots for the initial rinse, you can be boiling up a pot of sea water on the stove or fire. A squirt of saltwater soap will take care of any grease on your utensils or dishes. If you've had a particularly greasy meal, you may want to boil your utensils. Every few days, boiling the silverware is a good idea, in any event. Be careful about boiling your plastic bowls or cups, which may have a limited tolerance for such treatment. You can finish off your washing operation below the high-tide line on a sand or gravel beach. A rinse of your dishes with a little fresh water would be nice, and then towel them off with paper towels or Handi Wipes.

If you are camped up in the woods, or if washing on a rocky beach is going to create a hygienic or visual problem, you will need to dig yourself a little drain field. Get well away from your camp. A six- to ten-inch hole lined with a few rocks is the place to dump the gray water and the bits of food scraped off your plates and pots. When you finally break camp, shovel the dirt back into your little drain field. Getting rid of the residue of your meals, even the smell, not only is ecologically appropriate, but will also discourage the critters discussed earlier in the chapter, including the flies and bees that may be attracted.

# SAFETY, FIRST AID, AND REPAIRS

My earlier book, *Sea Kayaking Basics*, describes paddling skills, navigation and evasive maneuvers, as well as group and self-rescue techniques that make for safe kayakers and safe kayaking. There is no substitute for basic skills on the water, and the mastery of skills should be the first order of business for persons planning to go kayak camping. If you are going camping, you will usually be out in the elements longer, and there is the likelihood that you'll be straying farther from the handholds of civilization. In a sentence, be prepared to solve your own problems. We'll assume that you and your group possess the requisite paddling skills. What else do you need for a safe trip?

## SAFETY

Safety starts with a plan. That's how sea kayaking is quite different from its cousin, whitewater river running. Sea kayaking is 80 percent planning and 20 percent execution. River running is mostly execution. This cer-tainly does not mean that sea kayaking is "safer"; rather, you have an opportunity to make a plan that takes many objective factors into consideration with the idea of avoiding problems. Objective factors are those that can be measured or charted: time, distance, tides, currents, obstacles, shipping lanes, or eleva-tions—to mention a few. The biggest wild card in planning an outing is the weather—that's subjective, even chaotic—and what the wind and weather do usually bears some critical re-lationship to your objective factors. To simplify all of this, you want to make a plan that as-sumes a worst-case weather scenario, then asks if your itinerary is a prudent one for the skill level of your group, be it one or six per-sons. As I mentioned earlier, one approach to designing a safe trip is to plan around your weakest paddler and the longest crossing. It's on a crossing that wind and weather are likely to bring you to grief. A crossing is any piece of exposed water that takes you more than a hun-dred yards offshore, and that commits you and your crew to at least a mile, or more than fifteen minutes, of paddling.

The skill level of your group is also a matter of objective measurement, if you are realistic about it. In Chapter 2, we reproduced the rating system one club uses for its trips. The chart is really about the skills of the paddler. Go back and check it out, and try to be honest when setting an itinerary for your group.

Since weather is such an important factor, what are you going to do about it? There is probably no cape, no crossing, or narrows of nasty repute that can't be navigated with ease at some time, on some day of the year. But you can't plan for that. Likewise, certain areas by virtue of their large tides, strong currents, open fetches, cold waters, steep coastlines, and so forth are not going to meet your worst-case-weather-scenario test when matched against the composite skills of your group. You may have to settle for a less ambitious trip or a less ambitious route. It is possible to plan trips that have both a fair- and a foul-weather route. For example, the fair-weather routing might take you "outside," exposed to open ocean. But if wind and weather are not in your favor, you can take a route that keeps you in narrow passages between the islands and the mainland. In fact, every plan needs to be flexible when weather becomes unsettled. Sometimes, the best plan of all is to stay in camp, or delay a crossing or the rounding of a point until the winds fall. No matter where you paddle, the base-camp approach to camping (Chapter 2) tends to reduce your risks. In contrast, a point-to-point itinerary can lure an impatient group into trouble by committing paddlers to a route and a timetable. Trip planning should take into account the possibility of bad weather and should make provision for what happens if you can't keep to the schedule.

## WEATHER MATTERS

No matter when and where you go, take advantage of the weather services available to mariners. The best-known services are provided by the National Oceanic and Atmospheric Administration (NOAA). NOAA's marine forecasts, as well as other weather services, can be picked up on a VHF radio, and kayak campers shouldn't leave home without this vital piece of safety equipment. More valuable than a weather radio is a good nose for weather. People who spend a lot of time in the out-of-doors develop this naturally, so don't ignore some of the old saws repeated by outdoor books and old-timers since time immemorial: Mares' tails, a ring

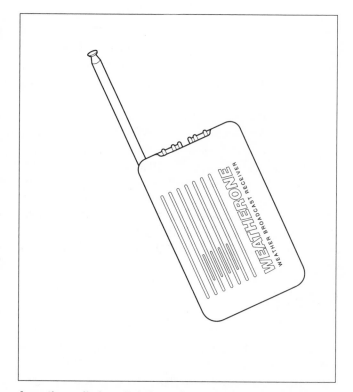

A weather radio is a vital piece of equipment for the kayaker.

around the sun, far objects appearing to float and be closer than they are, leaves on trees and bushes turning their backs, hyperactive birds—all might suggest rain in the next twenty four hours. "Red sky at night, sailor's delight; red sky in the morning, sailors take warning": Outdoor travelers claim it's true. Campfire smoke that rises straight up indicates high pressure and continued fair weather; smoke hovering near the ground suggests low pressure and approaching bad weather. Backing winds (counterclockwise) may bring bad weather in certain areas, while veering (clockwise) winds may be the pattern as the high, bringing fair weather, moves in. These and many more anomalies and local phenomena are worth paying attention to. Don't discount the claim of the old-timer in the hardware store who tells you his knee is acting up and "Bad weather's on the way"—he may have it just right!

## Wind

Very few weather forecasts deal with localized winds, those that are created by the interaction of sea and land mass or the shape of the topography itself. The former are convection winds created by the heating of the land mass during the day, which sucks the colder offshore air onshore, and especially up the valleys. Hence the frequent admonition to paddle early in the day, before the winds build. Onshore winds may at least take you in a direction you want to go—but don't count on it. Offshore winds, which can occur when cold, high-altitude air literally avalanches toward the sea, can cause real problems in certain parts of the world. My wife and I were warned of such a phenomenon as we embarked on a kayak trip up the Kona Coast of Hawaii, an area characterized by a hot, desert climate on the coast, rising to mountain rain

forests. In any part of the world, points of land, narrow inlets, and deep fjords can all act as wind compressors. These are also areas where ocean currents will accelerate. At least these are measurable, that is, objective, and often noted in your current tables or indicated on the charts. But neither the U.S. Weather Service nor NOAA is likely to warn you—on a day when the generalized wind forecast is moderate—about the twenty-five-mile-an-hour winds you'll encounter in Nasparti Inlet, or wherever.

## Fog

Fog can be a real problem in the marine environment. The morning fog with a yellow blob of sun and a blue cast from the sky above is convection fog, which usually burns off as the day progresses. Sea fogs, rolling in from offshore, are more persistent and are often accompanied by winds. The latter you may wish to avoid altogether. Making a so-called blind crossing in fog calls for good chart and compass skills, and any camping trip plan should count these as required equipment—whether or not you plan to undertake a blind crossing.

Whatever your itinerary, it's a good idea to file a float plan; at a minimum, that's letting friends, relatives, or co-workers know where you are planning to paddle and camp. Reproduced on the next page is an example of such a plan. Fill it out and leave it with friends; it's a simple form of insurance.

There are a number of precautions that aren't quite as glamorous as an Eskimo roll, but may be of more practical value. Tie your boat up, even if you're only leaving it for a short while. At night make sure the boats are well up on the beach, or even off the beach. Winds and tides don't give a hoot about your carefully crafted float plan. Hatch covers and spray

# OCEAN KAYAKING FLOAT PLAN

**Name and phone number of kayaker(s)**
**(Use back of sheet for additional persons.)**
1. _____  _____
2. _____  _____
3. _____  _____
4. _____  _____

**Descriptions of kayaks:**
**(Deck color, hull color, length)**
1. _____
2. _____
3. _____
4. _____

**Colors of expected paddling clothes:**
1. _____
2. _____
3. _____
4. _____

**Trip expectations:**
Put-in location: _____
Take-out location: _____
Approximate route: _____
Latest expected return date: _____

**If Overdue or in Case of Emergency,**
**Name & telephone of contact person:** _____  _____
Radio: AM/FM receiver          Shortwave receiver
Aircraft frequency transmitter     Marine band transmitter
ELT or EPIRB
Survival equipment: Tent style & color
First-aid kit          Spare paddle          Flares          Smoke
Panels          Weapons
Auto description/License #:
Where parked
Any other information

skirts can blow away and render your only means of transportation simply unseaworthy; make sure they are secure. A spare paddle, a tow rope, and duct tape are minimal accessories to prepare for the unexpected. Before setting out, dress for the worst anticipated conditions, and anticipate the worst. Always have warm clothing and foul-weather gear close at hand. A cold, wet paddler is a disabled paddler. Know where your next camp is, and have a Plan B or alternative if wind or weather makes progress difficult or unsafe. Not all the problems are on the water. Seaweed-covered rocks are more treacherous than the Matterhorn. These can do you in when you are landing, launching, or just taking a morning walk on the beach. Barnacle-covered rocks can carve you up like a sharp knife and do the same to the gel coat on your kayak; the banzai landing technique you use on sand is not a good idea here.

Boat and ship traffic is an underrated hazard. Especially at launch time, keep an eye out for passing tugs, ships, ferries—in fact, any boats that push up a huge wake. These miniature tidal waves can arrive, seemingly out of nowhere, as you prepare to launch and create more havoc than anything you'll encounter once you are on the water. Early in my sea-kayaking apprenticeship, I suffered the most serious mishap in years of canoe and kayak tripping. This personally embarrassing thrashing occurred early in the morning on a mirror-calm body of water in the Gulf Islands. The wake from a ferry en route from Swartz Bay to Tsawwassen, British Columbia, arrived at my rock-bound launch almost five minutes after the ferry plowed up the channel, a mile distant. I was swamped, tumbled. I banged my head on a rock, cut my hands on barnacles, bruised a shoulder, and lost a favorite hat. I have learned to check to seaward, no matter what my shore-line activity is, from washing dishes to launches and landings.

## FIRST AID

Let's assume that neither you nor any member of your crew has first aid or CPR training, and there is no doctor in your group. In other words, in the case of illness or injury, your principal challenge may be getting the victim to a place where he or she can be helped. Are you at any greater risk than a group setting off down the bike path or heading out for a two-night back-packing trip? A group of bikers is more likely to incur an injury, even a serious injury like a broken bone, but in their case car transportation is often near at hand, and an emergency room is probably close by. The backpackers are really in a less injury-prone environment than the bicyclists, but depending on the location, are likely to be farther from medical help in case of an injury. Sea kayakers off on a camping jaunt are in the same pickle as the backpackers, and seemingly the fact of being out on the water would put you farther from help. In fact, you are more likely to encounter motorized traffic on the water, including large boats with radio equipment; consequently, your victim may be much closer to medical help than the injured backpacker.

So at its simple level, first aid is about getting your victim to help in the fastest way possible. That's a factor to be considered in planning a trip, and the lack of any first-aid knowledge among your crew might make a difference in how far afield you wish to roam. As a practical matter, barring a human failure such as a heart or asthma attack or a severe toothache, the medical problems likely to occur on a sea-kayaking venture are somewhat predictable. Like the backpacker, you are most likely to come to grief on land or in the kitchen. Falling and in-

## NO ASSEMBLY REQUIRED: PREPACKAGED KITS

 Buying a prepackaged first-aid kit is easier and often less expensive than assembling your own. The following manufacturers offer prepackaged kits suitable for backcountry travel. Make sure your kit has enough of what you need, but not more than you can use effectively and legally.

• Emergency Medical Products, 9434 Chesapeake Dr., Suite 1208, San Diego, CA 92123; (800) 228-1538
• Adventure Medical Kits, P.O. box 2586, Berkeley, CA 94702; (206) 783-7107 (Seattle office)
• Emergency Systems, 1716 W. Main, Suite 8A, Bozeman, MT 59715; (406) 587-5571

## WILDERNESS MED SCHOOLS

In the backcountry, you can't rely on the concept of the "golden hour," which focuses on keeping victims alive during the hour or less required to deliver patients to a hospital. Rather, you have to be trained and prepared for situations that involve remote locations, prolonged transport, severe environments, and improvised equipment. Such training is intensive: For example, the Wilderness First Responder course offered by the National Association for Search and Rescue is 64 hours long (about 10 days) and costs about $100 including the textbook. Room and board are not included. The following organizations provide medical training intended specifically for people who spend time in the backcountry:

• National Association for Search and Rescue (affiliated with Wilderness Medical Associates), RFD2, Box 890, Brya Pond, ME 04219; (207) 665-2707
• SOLO, RR1, Box 163, Conway, NH 03818; (603) 447-6711
• Wilderness Medicine Institute, P.O. Box 9, Pitkin, CO 81241; (303) 641-3572.

The following compilation of first-aid materials is suitable for backcountry use by someone with WFR training or the equivalent. It is based on WMA's Expedition First-Aid Kit #1, or EFAK 1 (available for $100 from Emergency Medical Products in San Diego, (800) 228-1538), and is used with their permission. This is not your ordinary first-aid kit. Formal training is imperative to understanding what each of these items is for and how to use it properly. It's useless to carry anything in your kit that you're unfamiliar with. A kit such as this is only as effective as your knowledge and ability to apply it.

| General | Quantity | | | Dressings/Bandages | Quantity |
|---|---|---|---|---|---|
| *Tape, 1" | 1 | Plastic bag, large (for vapor barrier or weather protection) | 2 | Elastic bandages, 4" | 1 |
| Safety pins | 6 | Lubricating jelly (for inserting nasal airway) | 1 | Conforming gauze | 2 |
| Blanket pins | 2 | | | Roller bandage | 2 |
| Tongue depressor | 2 | Prep razor | 1 | *Triangle cravat | 2 |
| Nasal airway (for maintaining an open airway in semi-conscious patients) | 1 | Hemostat clamp (possible use: removing splinters) | 1 | Combine dressing | 2 |
| | | | | *Gauze, 4x4 | 6 |
| Syringe, 60cc (possible use: irrigating wounds with povidone-iodine solution) | 1 | Thermometer, regular | 1 | Lighter | 1 |
| | | Thermometer, low reading | 1 | *Soap | 1 |
| | | Gloves, nonsterile/sterile | 2 | *Light | 1 |
| Sam splint (for immobilizing injured areas) | 1 | Scalpel blade | 1 | Knife | 1 |

*(continued on next page)*

juring oneself on slippery rocks, beach logs, or while clambering up an embankment with a load is easy to do. Burns and cuts in the kitchen area are common. Incurring stings from bees or other insects or getting a stick in the eye are only slightly more prevalent than you'd expect at a family picnic. Burns from the sun, sun poisoning, blisters, and other skin irritations are common for kayak campers. Stomach and intestinal problems, including severe diarrhea, can be related to your kitchen—spoiled food or unsanitary utensils—or might result from tainted water or tainted shellfish. Consider the worst case: a capsize in cold waters with the victim having to be rescued or washed ashore after prolonged exposure.

## The First-Aid Kit

The scope of this book does not include instruction in first aid or wilderness medicine. For those of you who contemplate some ambitious tripping, the acquisition of first-aid and cardiopulmonary resuscitation (CPR) skills or Emergency Medical Training (EMT) would be smart. First Responder and American Red Cross advanced first-aid training offered in many communities should be researched. Otherwise, spend some time reading some of the excellent books avail-

able (see Appendix), and consider carrying a first-aid field manual. By all means, carry a good first-aid kit; the best ones contain simplified manuals. Familiarize yourself with the contents, and once you're under way, make sure the kit is in a place where you can get at it fast—not stuffed up into the bow of your kayak, for example.

A basic first-aid kit will carry bandages and dressings for topical or superficial cuts and abrasions, splints and dressings for more serious injuries, and a few nonprescription medicines. In the latter category are medicines for pain relief such as aspirin or ibuprofen, diarrhea control, decongestant and allergenic medicines, antihistamines for bites or stings, and an antacid for stomach problems. On pages 70–73 is a listing of items one might include in a comprehensive medical kit. Those items that represent the minimum requirement for a short outing have been starred.

Serious injuries—that is, injuries that require medical attention beyond the capabilities of the crew or the limitations of a simple first-aid kit—call for, at least, stabilization and immediate evacuation. The former may be no more than getting the victim into a supine position in a warm, dry place. If the victim cannot be moved,

| Emergency medicines | Quantity |
|---|---|
| Ammonia inhaler | 2 |
| (for certain unconscious and unresponsive victims) | |
| Epinephrine injectable | 1 |
| (for systemic allergic reactions such as those caused in some people by bee stings. Epinephrine is a prescription drug and its use requires training; ask your physician about it.) | |

| *Routine Materials | Quantity |
|---|---|
| Tincture of benzoin | 1 |
| (for treating skin so tape will stick) | |
| Petroleum jelly (Vaseline) | 1 |
| Alcohol swabs | 16 |
| Tape, 1" and 2" | 1 |
| Wound-closure strips | 1 |
| Adhesive strips, sterile (Band-Aids) | 20 |
| Gauze, 4x4 | 4 |
| Gauze, 2x2, (Telfa) | 8 |
| Adhesive dressing, 3x5 sheet | 1 |
| Magnifier | 1 |
| Cotton-tip applicators | 6 |

| | Quantity |
|---|---|
| Tongue depressor | 2 |
| Splinter forceps | 1 |
| Bandage scissors | 1 |
| Soap | 1 |

(continued on next page)

in the case of a severe break, the warm, dry environment must be created around, over, or under him or her. A serious back injury may preclude the latter.

Hypothermia is the ultimate complication resulting from prolonged immersion in cold water, and regardless of the degree of severity the treatment will be the same. A cold, shivering victim needs to be warmed, not just externally, but internally. The minimum treatment is to get the hypothermia victim into a sleeping bag and to ingest a hot fluid; soup is better than coffee. More advanced treatment may require the introduction of an external heat source, usually another body crawling into the sleeping bag with the victim.

But the ultimate objective is most likely to be evacuation. Flagging down passing motorized vessels would be the first, most obvious action. Many of the fancier pleasure boats out there have radios that may be used to summon help, even air evacuation in a very serious situation. In a remote location, where either commercial or pleasure boat traffic is rare, your options become limited. A victim could be placed in the bow of a double and paddled to the nearest phone or vehicle. The tow line could be used in very quiet water conditions. One paddler might be dispatched to find help. Needless to say, the scenarios are too variable to invite generalizations, so you, as trip leader, need to consider the crew, the destination, the itinerary, and have a catalog of possible emergencies and their antidotes in mind.

Prevention is always worth more than a boatload of cures. That can start with nothing more than physical fitness. Sounds simple, but the sad fact is that we are a society of unhealthy, unfit persons—and getting worse. Kayaking itself is a good activity for building aerobic and muscular fitness, but you need to develop some level of fitness before you take off onto the seas. The facts are plain: Fit persons are less likely to get sick and are less prone to accidents, and if they do sustain an injury or end up in the water, their recuperative and recovery powers are much greater than those of their less-fit companions.

Regardless of your fitness level, a physical and dental exam are a good form of pretrip insurance. Take care of any nagging problems that may be an annoyance around home, but could become real problems on a remote shore. Plan a trip that is appropriate to the health and fitness level of the group. The right clothing and the right shelter, designed to keep yourself warm and dry in any environment, are minimum insurance.

## Routine Medications   Quantity

| Medication | Quantity |
|---|---|
| * Acetaminophen (Tylenol) (a minor analgesic, or pain reliever; has less tendency than aspirin to irritate the stomach) | 20 |
| * Aspirin, 325 mg (like acetaminophen, reduces fever as well as relieving minor pain) | 20 |
| * Antacid tablets (for indigestion) | 12 |
| * Bismuth subsalicylate (Pepto-Bismol) (for diarrhea) | 12 |
| * Syrup of Ipecac, 30cc (to induce vomiting in victims of certain poisoning) | 1 |
| Activated charcoal (in case of certain types of poisoning) | 1 |
| * Decongestant, topical, 1 oz. (Oxymetazoline) | 1 |
| Benzocaine dental analgesic (Orabase) | 1 |
| Dextromethorphan (Robitussin DM) (for coughs) | 10 |
| Diphenhydramine, 25 mg (Benadryl) (an antihistamine for mild allergic reactions) | 8 |
| * Ibuprofen, 200 mg (Advil, Nuprin) (a minor analgesic with anti-inflammatory properties) | 16 |
| Otic solution (for ears) | 1 |
| Povidone-iodine ointment, 10%, 1 oz. (as an antiseptic for cleaning skin and wounds) | 1 |
| Pseudoephedrine, 30 mg, (Sudafed) (a systemic decongestant) | 1 |

*(continued on next page)*

Hats, sunglasses, sunblock creams, and lip protection should be a part of your essential outfit. Making provisions for hygienic camping—dishwashing, bathing, human-waste disposal, and pure water —can forestall the invisible villains.

Finally, don't relax just because you've landed and are off the water. Just as in everyday life, most accidents happen close to home—in this case, camp. I have no statistics, but based on anecdotal evidence and personal experience, the most common injuries are strains, pulls, even herniated disks from hauling loaded kayaks or heavy gear packs to and from a launch site. The next most common mishaps are falls occurring during the same activity. You can take your own precautions to minimize these land-based hazards. Here's a simple example of injury insurance: If you are going to move a couple of loaded kayaks up the beach, organize four people to do the task instead of two persons straining their backs. Better yet, completely unload the boats first; then two persons can easily move the kayaks.

# REPAIRS

Taking care of the humans in your group is, of course, the most important thing. But you've got a lot of equipment that you are depending upon, too. Boats and paddles are all you've got to get you to and from your destination, so make sure these are shipshape before you leave. It's easier to repair a boat or paddle in your garage than in the field. A day or weekend trip as a shakedown cruise to ferret out defective or missing equipment is a good idea.

In the field, at a minimum, you want tapes and adhesives that can effect quick, simple repairs. It's inelegant, but duct tape (buy the best quality you can find) can be used to repair all but the most disastrous breaks, cracks, or holes in a boat hull—regardless of its material. Plastic boats are almost indestructible, so a broken or leaking kayak is more than likely to be made of glass. A fiberglass patch kit consisting of glass cloth, resin and hardening agent, a tongue depressor, paper cup, and sandpaper would be wise to take on an extended trip, but duct tape will suffice for any short adventures. Waterproof adhesives or "goops" like Shoe Goo can be used for a variety of repairs: small holes or boat cracks, damaged gum boots, torn neoprene spray skirts or torn sandals. An epoxy kit from the hardware store is good repair insurance for various boat hardware or for securing a loose joint—usually

| | | |
|---|---|---|
| Tolnaftate (Tinactin) (for athlete's foot) | 1 | **Optional** |
| Zinc oxide * (as a sun block) | 1 | Meclizine, 25 mg, (Bonine) (for motion sickness) Calamine cream (for poison ivy) |
| Stool softener, DSS/DCS (for constipation) | 20 | |
| Laxative suppositories (Bisacodyl; Dulcolax) (for constipation) | 10 | To these items add signaling gear, such as a mirror, flares, EPIRB, and a VHF radio. |
| Fluorescein dye strips (for use with eye injuries) | 2 | |

**Reprinted with permission from *Canoe & Kayak* magazine.**

the inner sleeve—in a two-piece paddle. Tape, cord, and soft wire can be brought to bear on a huge array of repairs. A few adhesives can take care of the rest.

The simplest tools should be on board: gooseneck pliers can double as a pot grabber in the kitchen and a repair tool for your boat; a knife, screwdriver, awl, and small file—indeed, no more than the tools on a good Swiss Army knife—will handle virtually every conceivable repair problem you might face. If your boat has specialized hardware, attachments, and a rudder, consider a kit that includes replacement nuts, bolts, cotter pins, rivets, and the necessary tools for working them. Lubricants—I carry 3-In-One oil—can be used for everything from knife-sharpening stones, to sticky rudder pedals, to coating the blade on the fillet knife for saltwater protection. Finally, consider repairs for tents, tarps, and clothing. Patching materials, adhesives, grommet kits, and sewing kits are available for every conceivable rip, tear, or dismemberment suffered by your camping gear.

As we did with the first-aid kit, we provide a complete repair-kit list on page 88. You can pick and choose among the items listed, with your choices dictated by the length and difficulty of your trip, and an assessment of the condition of the fleet.

# 9

# TAKING THE KIDS

Enjoying outdoor activities with your kids seems like a too-obvious suggestion. You probably already know a hundred reasons why you would all like to get away from the yard work, schoolwork, work-work, and the mall. As a more practical matter, you may also realize that if the kids can't go, you can't go—unless, of course, you're paid up on the nanny's social security and workers' comp taxes.

Less obvious is the fact that you need to get the kids in on the action early in life. Don't wait until their teens. By that time, they'll have a more pressing agenda than going camping with Mom and Dad. How early? We don't exaggerate when we suggest that you think about including kids as soon as they are out of diapers. The real limiting factor is your own level of competence. You must be confident of your skills, and you must observe the maxim about planning your trip around the weakest member of the group.

A base-camp type of itinerary is obviously desirable where kids are concerned. Unlike goal-oriented adults who may measure the success of a trip by the numbers of miles covered, campsites set, and points of interest cataloged, kids just want to "get there" and start making sand castles or skipping rocks. It is not, in fact, the journey; it's the destination! As an adult, you may learn by including the kids to slow down a bit and to enjoy the small but beautiful aspects of camping on rivers, lakes, and oceans. What the kids learn is how to enjoy themselves in the natural world, which provides its own light shows and sights and sounds without electronics.

On a recent weekend trip in Washington State's San Juan Islands we watched a group of subteen boys who had arrived in double kayaks, teamed up with their parents, spend over two hours paddling and poling log "canoes" around the small protected bay where we were camped. They were mastering boat and paddle skills that could not be duplicated in a week at a canoe camp. At dusk, they beached their fleet and set about thoroughly exploring no more than one hundred yards of coastline on foot as their parents prepared dinner on the bluff above. The point is that most kids don't really need Nintendo to amuse themselves.

Let's assume your own skills are above average and you feel confident about including young children in the boats. The first question is where to put them. Some kayaks—either singles or doubles—are better suited to adding nonpaddling children than others. There are a number of very-large-volume doubles on the market, for which the center hatch can be adapted to take a small child. Some recent designs are equipped with a third-person center hatch—adult or child. If a car seat can be fitted into a hatch you've got a good start, especially if your kid is used to sitting in a car seat.

Another spot for the smallest children is in your lap, but you may find that it's difficult to paddle with a kid's head where the paddle shaft wants to be. Yet another option is the front or rear hatch. The rear hatch is larger, but you and the child can't see each other. That could make both of you uncomfortable, unless you have a trailing kayak to keep eye contact. The front hatch makes more sense, but many are too small to accommodate a passenger. The magical time is when your child is big enough to wield a paddle from the bow of a double kayak. Depending upon the child's age, strength, and—more important—attention span, you'll want to manage the distance between rest stops and diversions extremely carefully. Shorter is better! The next progression, for really committed families and strong paddlers, is a solo kayak for a youngster. Recently introduced touring kayak models designed for women would certainly be suitable for kids in the 80- to 120-pound range.

Regardless of their age, taking the kids has been made easier in recent years by the introduction of specific kid-sized gear and clothing. PFDs for infants, children, and juniors are now widely available. There are paddles sized for kids, too. Quality rain gear, footwear, and other outdoor clothing is available in greater variety than ever

before. Patagonia, for example, has a separate catalog for kids. Here's another thought for those of you with high-level paddling and outdoor skills who may want to take very young kids on more aggressive adventures: One couple of our acquaintance has done some ambitious coastal cruising with their five-year-old. In addition to a PFD, their boy wears a tiny neoprene wet suit. The center hatch of their kayak is superlarge. Their son sits on carefully arranged duffel, and a

Dressing a child for a role as inactive passenger: shorty wet suit and PFD

specially designed spray skirt keeps him dry. Whether your kid's "nest" is a seat or duffel, you want the child as low in the boat as possible, but not so low that he or she can't see what's going on. And you don't want the child on the floor of the kayak, which is likely to be a cold, wet place.

Keeping the kids warm and dry is, in fact, your primary challenge, especially in an environment that wants to thwart your best efforts. Kids seem less able to monitor and regulate their personal thermostats than adults. An adult will put on a sweater and a hat before her lips turn blue; but a ten-year-old will be shivering uncontrollably in his shirtsleeves before everyone realizes he's verging on hypothermia. Also consider the level of activity of a child who is a passenger compared with your own as you paddle vigorously. You are warm in a polypro shirt; your child needs to be bundled up in a rain parka, shirt, and sweater with a hat on his or her head.

One of our early, pleasant discoveries was that nonpaddling kids in a canoe or kayak fall asleep within moments after getting under way. There is something soporific about the tinkle of wavelets against a boat hull. It's better than a glass of warm milk. But food is the other magic ingredient for happy young campers. Whether you're in the boat or in camp, having plenty of finger foods at the ready is smart planning. We are all for healthy diets, and outdoor appetites will invite you to make cooking a priority activity for kayak camping. But for the kids, we're talking about between-meal snacks. It may not be health food, but nothing solves the riddle of "When will we be there?" better than a fistful of M&M's or Cracker Jack.

Another interesting challenge is how to arrange for the kids' sleeping. They tend to be more athletic than their parents, and after just a few acrobatics they are off their sleeping pads and onto the tent floor—all too often into the puddle in the corner. The new synthetics for sleeping bags have mitigated many of the problems we used to experience with down or flannel bags, whether from dampness or bed wetting or the accidental dunking. Also, there are now bags on the market that can actually be expanded as the kids grow. We started off by having the youngest children share the tent with us; later, our two daughters graduated to their own two-person tent. You need to have a high tolerance for chaos. If you think your kids are sloppy at home, you haven't seen anything until you've seen what two kids can do to the inside of a tent! The chaos may be a source of amusement for the most part—that is, until the rains come, and the sleeping bags and clothing are scattered helter-skelter about the tent and against the walls, with the doors half zippered. When the weather turns nasty, you may have to get involved in some maintenance and damage control.

There was an article in an outdoor magazine recently about a family on a canoe trip in the Boundary Waters Canoe Area of Minnesota, which described virtually every trial and tribulation that could befall parents trying to get their two kids through a week's camping experience. No manner of paddling, portaging, feeding, tenting, or wardrobe-management activity came easy. But the clear message of the story was that the rewards far outweighed the difficulties, and the title of the article said it all: "Unconditional Love."

This is hardly a definitive manual on taking kids on a kayak-camping adventure, but is meant simply to encourage you to develop your own capabilities so that you can include them. Usually, local canoe and kayak clubs are the best place to meet other families with whom to paddle, and members who can provide advice and support. The rewards of making your kayak camping a family affair are substantial, and you will undoubtedly be preparing your kids for the adoption of a lifelong sport for their own adulthood.

# SELF-SUPPORT RIVER RUNNING

An earlier chapter described the touring kayak as a "backpack on the water," and a very large one at that. Even the small, British-style sea kayaks can carry a substantial load. The most space-constrained kayaker is the whitewater river runner, and *self-support* is a term used to distinguish the kayakers who carry everything they need for a multiday trip in their boats from those who travel in a group accompanied by large rafts. The rafts, with their huge capacity, become the pack horses for the kayaks—and everyone else for that matter. Whitewater river running, with its specialized skills, may not be within your current aspirations, but there is little essential difference between the pleasures sought by river runners on a kayak camping trip and those enjoyed by coastal cruisers. For many of us, any mode of water or boat is a great excuse to get outdoors. What we can learn from the self-supported river runner is just how little is really necessary to go camping out of a kayak.

Much emphasis in this book has been put on being comfortable, and you have been treated to long lists of food, clothing, camping gear, food, and utensils. In fact, you might conclude that comfort was somehow synonymous with more. The facts may be otherwise. I interviewed Bob McDougall, a world adventurer—now a marketing manager for Patagonia—on the subject of self-support. McDougall has an extraordinary résumé of first descents and river-running exploits on this continent and beyond. Self-support trips are not a matter of deprivation or special challenge, in his view; rather, they provide the real freedom that many of us are searching for. In his mind, it is the lack of encumbrances that enhances our experience.

McDougall has taken self-supported trips lasting from a more typical five to six days to river explorations lasting twenty days. For the latter, or in fact any trip beyond a week, food capacity is the limiting factor, and arrangements must be made for food drops or reprovisioning. Such trips would be the exception, indeed, since there are barely a handful of long, remote whitewater rivers left in our modern world.

Some whitewater kayaks have more space than others, and regardless of whether or not you stuff every last cubic inch of your kayak with food and gear, the greater the volume of your kayak, the less effect any size load is going to have on the boat's performance. Some whitewater kayaks manufactured by Prijon do not have vertical pillars—foam supports usually running from behind the seat into the point of the stern and from the front of the cockpit into the bow peak—which theoretically provides more space for the self-supported paddler. Most other boats do have pillars, and I have heard boaters talking about temporarily removing these in order to make additional room for self-support trips.

"Nonsense," avers McDougall. "I've never removed the pillars from a boat, but I did have to cut a small piece out of one in order to accommodate a video camera on one of our trips." McDougall does not consider his outfit to be the paddler's equivalent of the hair shirt, but he does revel in the challenge of making do with the minimal, but right, stuff. He likes to spread out all of his chosen gear, and then make a final cut of any item that is even slightly redundant.

As you might expect, sleeping well is always a necessity, so an ultralight, synthetic-fill sleeping bag is the first item. We described such a bag in Chapter 6. You can use your PFD as a sleeping pad, but here, McDougall prefers the comfort of the Therm-a-Rest (smallest size) air mat, which stuffs nicely into the very peak of the kayak. A ten-by-twelve tarp supported by cord and the kayak paddles—in the absence of other anchor points—is the usual shelter, but in rainy parts of the world he might carry a small bivy sack. He never carries a tent; the weight is out of proportion to the shelter value.

McDougall gets almost all of his food at the supermarket and it runs predominantly to the high-carbohydrate, bulk concentrated foodstuffs like pasta, Top Ramen, cereals, and breads. The bread is the ubiquitous bagel. Would he forgo a morning cup of coffee because it has no food value? "No way; I enjoy a little jump-start in the morning, even if it's the powdered variety." In fact, the meals are planned around one pot. In McDougall's case it may be a coffee can with a wire laced though the top. Whatever water doesn't get used to reconstitute the pasta or make the tea is used to clean the pot, cup, and utensil(s). His plastic drinking cup and eating bowl may be one and the same. The utensil other than a spoon is the blade on a small Swiss Army knife, which is also his principal repair tool. He rarely carries a stove. Short trips include mostly foods that can be eaten without cooking. A small fire can takes care of every other cooking need. Short-trip foods would include bagels, cheese, fruit, and, yes, PowerBars. The latter are the energy bars much in favor among endurance athletes like cyclists and triathletes, and they are, in fact, highly concentrated, nutritious, and tasty. In or out of their foil wrapper they are also waterproof; I often carry one in the little outside pocket on my PFD, which was probably put there to carry the car keys.

Clothing needs will depend upon the climate: warm and dry with relatively warm water; or cold, wet areas with cold waters. For the former, a dry top paddling jacket (that's one with latex gaskets at wrists and neck) over a long-sleeve Capilene or polypro shirt, and a pair of shorts provide most of the clothing, in or out of the boat. For the latter, a wet or dry suit is usually necessary. In either climate, a lightweight pile sweater would be the principal garment for warmth, and in cold, wet areas the pants would be Capilene or other synthetic, hydrophobic long johns. Rain and wind protection can come from a paddling jacket, but a dry top is too uncomfortable; otherwise, the lightest weight nylon shell is the answer. McDougall's footwear of choice is tennis shoes rather than neoprene booties, since the fabric shoes can be dried out and you can walk or hike in them; the booties always feel clammy and are almost useless for walking. A warm Synchilla hat is a final item of clothing favored by McDougall for taking care of the evening chill in almost any climate.

Does this last of the breed need to carry a flashlight? You bet! "It doesn't have to be *War and Peace*, but I always carry a book, and I carry a small headlamp to read by. Many of our trips have been to third world countries where our book and our light were the only shreds of civilized life."

McDougall packs his sleeping bag in a separate waterproof stuff bag and pushes his Therm-a-Rest mat into the stern of his kayak. Waterproof bags of different shapes and sizes can be used for the rest of the gear that needs to be kept dry, or you can use stow floats. Several manufacturers (Voyageur, Stohlquist, Pacific Water Sports) offer variations on the theme. These are tapered tubes of waterproof nylon or vinyl with either zipper, roll-up, Velcro, or buckle (or a combination) closures. When not being used for gear stowage, they are inflated to serve as the rear flotation, a necessary accessory for all whitewater kayaks, or for any kayak that lacks watertight bulkheads. When they are used as gear bags, the practice is to stuff them, then force all of the air out of them before plugging them into the kayak.

It's a good practice in any kayak, but especially important in a whitewater kayak, to get as much weight near the center of the kayak—that is, behind the seat—as possible. The lighter gear gets stuffed toward the ends of the boat. McDougall puts all of his gear in the rear of the boat and behind the seat, nothing in the bow (by the way, McDougall is six foot four—no shrimp!). He also favors a boat in which the seat can be moved forward to compensate for the load in the rear. This is a standard feature in many kayaks, but requires some special adaptation or alteration in others.

*Freedom* is the word McDougall uses to describe the self-support kayaker with minimal gear. Even if you never expect to find yourself on a whitewater river, consider the message. You can be warm, comfortable, well fed, and *free* with a minimum of paraphernalia.

# APPENDIX

# BOOKS

## Instruction and General

Burch, David. *Fundamentals of Kayak Navigation*. Chester, Conn.: Globe Pequot Press, 1987. 283 pp. Bibl. Index.

Diaz, Ralph. *Complete Folding Kayaker*. Camden, Me.: Ragged Mountain Press, 1994. 162 pp. Illus. Index.

Dowd, John. *Sea Kayaking: A Manual for Long-distance Touring*, rev. ed. Vancouver, B.C.: Douglas & McIntyre; Seattle: University of Washington Press, 1988. 303 pp. Illus. Bibl. Index.

Harrison, David. *Sea Kayaking Basics*. New York: Hearst Marine Books, 1993. 125 pp. Illus. Bibl. Index.

Hutchinson, Derek C. *Hutchinson's Guide to Sea Kayaking*. Chester, Conn.: Globe Pequot Press, 1985. 122 pp. Illus. Index.

Hutchinson, Derek. *Eskimo Rolling*. Camden, Me.: International Marine Publishing, 1988. 152 pp. Illus. Index.

Seidman, David. *The Essential Sea Kayaker: A Complete Course for the Open Water Traveler*. Camden, Me.: International Marine Publishing, 1992. 144 pp. Illus.

Washburne, Randel. *The Coastal Kayaker's Manual: A Complete Guide to Skills, Gear, and Sea Sense*. Chester, Conn.: Globe Pequot Press, 1989. 226 pp. Illus. Bibl. Index.

## Guidebooks

Carey, Neil G. *A Guide to the Queen Charlotte Islands*. Anchorage: Alaska Northwest Publishing, 1975–. Annual.

DuFresne, Jim. *Glacier Bay National Park*. Seattle: The Mountaineers, 1987. 152 pp. Illus. Maps.

Horwood, Dennis, and Tom Parkin. *Islands for Discovery: An Outdoor Guide to B.C.'s Queen Charlotte Islands*. Victoria, B.C.: Orca Book Publishers, 1989. 200 pp. Illus. Maps.

Ince, John, and Heidi Kottner. *Sea Kayaking Canada's West Coast*. Vancouver, B.C.: Raxas Books, 1982. 240 pp. Illus. Maps. Index.

Miller, David William. *A Guide to Alaska's Kenai Fjords*, 2d ed. Cordova, Alaska: Wilderness Images, 1987. 116 pp. Illus. Bibl. Index.

Snowden, Mary Ann. *Island Paddling: A Paddler's Guide to the Gulf Islands and Barkley Sound*. Victoria, B.C.: Orca Publishers, 1990. 200 pp. Illus.

Sutherland, Chuck, ed. *Northeastern Coastal Paddling Guide*. Tuckahoe, N.Y.: Association of North Atlantic Kayakers, 1984. 39 pp. Illus. Maps.

Washburne, Randel. *The Coastal Kayaker: Kayak Camping on the Alaska and B.C. Coast*. Seattle: Pacific Search Press, 1983. 214 pp. Illus. Maps. Bibl. Index.

Washburne, Randel. *Kayaking Puget Sound, the San Juans, and Gulf Islands: 45 Trips on the Northwest's Inland Waters*. Seattle: The Mountaineers, 1990. 224 pp. Illus. Bibl.

Washburne, Randel. *Kayak Trips in Puget Sound and the San Juan Islands*. Seattle: Pacific Search Press, 1986. 153 pp. Illus. Maps. Bibl.

Weaverling, Charles K. *Kayak Routes and Camping Beaches in Western and Central Prince William Sound, Alaska*. 1987. Available from Wild Rose Guidebooks.

Ziegler, Ronald. *Wilderness Waterways: A Whole Water Reference for Paddlers*. Kirkland, Wash.: Canoe America Associates, 1991. 177 pp. (Bibliography and source book for most of the entries in this Appendix)

## Survival and First Aid

Bettsworth, Michael. *Drownproofing: A Technique for Water Survival*. New York: Schocken Books, 1977.

Breyfogle, Newell. *Commonsense Outdoor Medicine and Emergency Companion*. Blue Ridge Summit, Pa.: Ragged Mountain Press, 3rd edition, 1993.

Craighead, Frank C., and John J. Craighead. *How to Survive on Land and Sea*. Annapolis, Md.: Naval Institute Press, 1984.

Forgey, William W., M.D. *Hypothermia: Death by Exposure*. Merrillville, Ind.: ICS Books, 1985.

Forgey, William W., M.D. *Wilderness Medicine: Beyond First Aid*. Merrillville, Ind.: ICS Books, 1987.

Hayward, J. S. *The Nature and Treatment of Hypothermia*. Minneapolis: University of Minnesota Press, 1983.

Isaac, Jeff, P.A.C., and Peter Goth, M.D. *The Outward Bound Wilderness First-Aid Handbook*. New York: Lyons & Burford, 1991.

Keatinge, W. R. *Survival in Cold Water*. Oxford, U.K.: Blackwell Scientific Publications, 1969.

Shanks, Bernard. *Wilderness Survival*. New York: Universe Books, 1980.

Tilton, Buck, M.S. *Backcountry First Aid and Extended Care*, 2d ed. Merrillville, Ind.: ICS Books, 1994.

Tilton, Buck, M.S. *Medicine for the Backcountry*, 2d ed. Merrillville, Ind.: ICS Books, 1994.

Tilton, Buck, M.S., and Steve Griffin. *First Aid for Youths*. Merrillville, Ind.: ICS Books, 1994.

## MAGAZINES

*Atlantic Coastal Kayaker*
29 Burley St.
Wenham, MA 01984

*Canoe & Kayak*
P.O. Box 3146
Kirkland, WA 98083
1-800-MY CANOE

*Folding Kayaker*
P.O. Box 0754
Planetarium Station
New York, NY 10024

*Kayak Touring*
P.O. Box 3146
Kirkland, WA 98083
1-800-MY CANOE

*Paddler Magazine*
4061 Oceanside Blvd., Suite M
Oceanside, CA 92056
(303) 879-1450

*Sea Kayaker*
6327 Seaview Ave. N.W.
Seattle, WA 98107-2664
(206) 789-7350

# ORGANIZATIONS

ANORAK (Association of North Atlantic Kayakers)
34 East Queens Way
Hampton, VA 23669

Maine Island Trail Association
P.O. Box 8, 41A Union Wharf
Portland, ME 04101

TASK (Trade Association of Sea Kayaking)
P.O. Box 84144
Seattle, WA 98124

Washington Water Trails Association
4649 Sunnyside Ave. North #345
Seattle, WA 98103-6900

# MAPS AND CHARTS

**Environment Canada, Canadian Hydrographic Service Institute of Ocean Sciences**
P.O. Box 8080
Ottawa, ON K1G 3H6
(613) 998-4931
Charts for all the Great Lakes and Canadian coastal waters.

**National Oceanic and Atmospheric Administration**
National Ocean Service, Distribution Branch
Riverside, MD 20737-1191
(301) 436-6990
Publishes charts for waters surrounding the United States and its possessions. A free index is available. NOAA also publishes a series of United States Coast Pilots.

**United States Geological Survey**
National Mapping Division
National Center
12201 Sunrise Valley Dr.
Reston, VA 22092
(703) 648-6131
Free index. Topographic maps useful for coastal areas where land features (like trails, roads, etc.) are important to an itinerary.

## Nongovernment Sources and Dealers

**American Nautical Services Navigation Center**
514 Biscayne Blvd.
Miami, FL 33132
(305) 358-1414
Chart dealer.

**Bahai Mar Marine Store**
801 Seabreeze Blvd.
Fort Lauderdale, FL 33316
(305) 764-8831
Chart dealer.

**Baker, Lyman and Co.**
3220 1-10 Service Rd. W.
Metairie, LA 70001
(504) 831-3685
8876 Gulf Fwy., Suite 110
Houston, TX 77007
(713) 943-7032
Chart dealer.

**Bovey Marine Ltd.**
375 Water St.
Vancouver, BC V6B 3J5
(604) 685-8216
Chart dealer.

**Boxells Chandlery**
68 Long Wharf
Boston, MA 02110
(617) 523-5678
Chart dealer.

**W. T. Brownley Co.**
118 W. Plume St.
Norfolk,VA 23510
(804) 622-7589
Chart dealer.

**Captains Nautical Supplies**
138 N.W. 10th St.
Portland, OR 97209
(503) 227-1648
1914 Fourth Ave.
Seattle, WA 98101
(800) 448-2278
Chart dealer.

**Dominion Map Ltd.**
541 Howe St.
Vancouver, BC V6C 2Z1
(604) 684-4341
Mapmaker, map dealer.

**Gabriel Aero Marine Instruments**
1490 Lower Water St.
Halifax, NS B3J 2R7
(902) 423-7252
351 St. Paul St. W
Montreal, PQ H2Y 2A7
(514) 845-8342
Chart dealer.

**McCurnin Nautical Charts Co.**
2318 Woodlawn Ave.
Metairie, LA 70001
(504) 888-4500
Chart dealer.

**McGill Maritime Services**
369 Place d'Youville
Montreal, PQ H2Y 2G2
(514) 849-1125
Chart dealer.

**Maritime Services Ltd.**
3440 Bridgewater St.
Vancouver, BC V5K 1B6
(604) 294-4444
Chart dealer.

**Maryland Nautical Sales**
1143 Hull St.
Baltimore, MD 21230
(301) 752-4268
Chart dealer.

**New York Nautical Instrument
and Service Corp.**
140 W. Broadway
New York, NY 10013
(212) 962-4522
Chart dealer.

**Ocean River Sports**
1437 Store St.
Victoria BC, V8W 3J6
(604) 381-4233
Chart dealer.

**Pacific Map Center**
647 Auahi St.
Honolulu, HI 96813
(808) 531-3800
Chart dealer.

**Safe Navigation Inc.**
107 E. 8th St.
Long Beach, CA 90813
(213) 590-8744
Chart dealer.

**Southwest Instruments Co.**
235 W. 7th St.
San Pedro, CA 80731
(213) 519-7800
Chart dealer.

**Tradewind Instruments Ltd.**
2540 Blanding Ave.
Alameda, CA 94501
(415) 523-5726
Chart dealer.

# CLUBS, ASSOCIATIONS, NEWSLETTERS

## Alaska
**Knik Kanoers and Kayakers Inc.**
c/o Jeanne Molitor
P.O. Box 101935
Anchorage, AK 99510
(907) 272-9351

## British Columbia
**British Columbia Kayak and Canoe Club**
1606 W. Broadway
Vancouver, BC, Canada V6S 1S8

## California
**Bay Area Sea Kayakers**
c/o Penny Wells
229 Courtright Rd.
San Rafael, CA 94901
(415) 457-6094

## Florida
**Florida Sea Kayaking Association**
c/o George Ellis
3095 67th Ave. S.
St. Petersburg, FL 33172
(813) 864-2651

## Georgia
**Coastal Georgia Paddling Club**
c/o Katie Goodwin
505 Herb River Dr.
Savannah, GA 31406

## Hawaii
(Virtually every town and village in Hawaii has an outrigger canoe club; and most members paddle surf skis.)

## New York
**Metropolitan Association of Sea Kayakers**
c/o Al Ysaguirre
195 Prince St.
New York, NY 10012

## Texas
**Texas Sea/Touring Kayak Club**
P.O. Box 27281
Houston, TX 77227
(Sherry Gillan: [713] 660-7000)

## Washington
**Washington Kayak Club**
c/o Kathy Anderson
P.O. Box 24264
Seattle, WA 98124
(206) 788-7919

# EQUIPMENT CHECKLIST

### Boat Accessories
Paddle and spare
Spray skirt
Life jacket (PFD)
Bilge pump
Sponge
Painter (bowline)
Flotation
Storage bags
Paddle float or sponsons
Rope for rescues, stirrup
Sea anchor
Sail or kit

### Navigational Equipment
Charts and map case
Current and tide tables
Compass
Binoculars
Weather radio

### Repair Kit
Duct tape
Soft wire
Pliers
Light oil, WD-40
Swiss Army knife
Fiberglass patch kit (cloth, resin, catalyst)
Hull patch kit (for folding boats)

### Emergency Equipment
Flares or signaling device
Emergency Position Indicating Radio Beacon (EPIRB)
VHF or CB transmitter

### Survival Equipment
Wet suit or dry suit
Whistle
Waterproof matches and fire starter
High-energy food bars
Tea or bouillon
Personal shelter (tarp, space blanket, etc.)

### First-Aid Kit
Painkiller
Seasickness pills
Ace bandage
Sterile compresses
Gauze roll
Butterfly closures
Triangular bandages
Adhesive tape
Safety pins
Fast-acting laxative and emetic
Aspirin
Antibiotics
Burn ointment
Tweezers
Scissors
First-aid book

## Clothing

Fast-drying pants (extra pair)
Wool or pile pants
Long underwear
Polypropylene undershirt
Wool or pile shirt
Sweater
Vest (synthetic fill)
Wool or pile hat
Broad-brimmed rain hat
Rain parka and pants
Paddling gloves or mitts (pogies)
Rubber boots (wading height)
Sandals, footwear for walking ashore

## Camping Equipment

Tent and fly
Rain tarp
Sleeping bag, plus stuff and waterproof bag
Sleeping mat
Towel
Lighter or matches

Saw and small ax
Insect repellent
Toilet paper
Flashlight
Candles or lantern
Toilet kit
Sun shower
Dry bags for clothing and equipment
Mesh duffel and tote bags
Camera bag or box
Fishing gear

## Cooking Equipment

Cook kit and pans
Stove and fuel
Eating and serving utensils
Dish soap and scrubbers
Cup
Spices
Food storage bags
Water containers (large and personal)
Water purifier

# INDEX

Hudson River, x
Hygiene, 5, 37, 46, 48, 63, 64, 73
Hypothermia, 72, 77

Injury, *see* First Aid
Itinerary, 75; *see also* Float Plan; Planning

Kauai (Hawaii), 12
Kayak camping, complexity of, 5
Kayaks: as backpack, 1; British style, ix, 3; double sea, 3, *3*; fat, 18–19; folding, 13; fishing and, 63; hauling capacity of, 2, 9; lakes and, 9–10; load distribution and, 4; multipurpose, 17; packing of, 20–21; racks for, 22; rivers and, 3, 79–81; sea, 17, *18*; sizes compared, 3–4, 17; skinny, 17–18, *18*, 20; special, 19; stability of, 63; storage capacity of, 2; storage of, 20; transporting of, 20–22; tripping vessel, described, 19–20; wheels for, *21*, 22; whitewater, ix, *2*, 17, 20, 80, 81; *see also* Sea Kayaks; brand names
*Kayak Touring*, 10
Kids, 75–77; kayak seating for, 76, 77; paddling and, 76, 77; PFD's for, 76; sleeping arrangement for, 77
Kitchens, camping, 47; example of, *52*; location of, 51; shopping trip for, 59; utensils, 57, 58
Klepper (kayak), 19
Knots, lines and, *42, 43*, 43–44
KOA, 47
Kona Coast (Hawaii), 8, 67

Lake Canyon (Utah), 13
Lake Powell (Utah), 13
Lakes, kayaks and, 9–10
Lake Superior, 10, 11
Lake Winnipeg, 9
Landing, 35, 36
Launching, 35

Life preserver, *see* PFD
Light sources: candles, 46; flashlights, 46, 81; gasoline, 46; hazards of, 46; headlamp, *45*, 81; lanterns, *45*, 46, 47; penlight, *45*, 46; propane, 46
Lines, *see under* Knots
Little Na Pali Coast (Hawaii), 12

McDougall, Bob, 79, 80, 81
Mackenzie River (Canada), 9
Magazines, 85–86; *see also under* titles
Magdalena Bay (Baja California), 12
Maine Island Trail, 8
Maine Island Trail Association, 10
*Maine Island Trail Guidebook*, 33
Manhattan Island, x
Manitoba, 9
Maps and charts, 15, 86–87
Marin Headlands (San Francisco Bay), 12
Matches, 56
Matresses, *see* Beds; Therm-a-Rest
Medications, 71, 72–73; *see also* First Aid
Menus, 58; *see also* Food; Kitchens
Mesh-top shoes, *see under* Footwear
Mexico, 10, 12
Meyer, Kathleen, *How to Shit in the Woods*, 49
Minnesota, 11
Missouri River (Montana), 8
Moisture evaporation (sweat), 23, 25
Montana, 8
Mosqui Canyon (Utah), 13
Mosquitoes, 39
Mountaineers (kayak club), 6
Mountain goats, 12
Muscle Ridge Channel (Maine), 10

Nasparti Inlet, 67
*National Geographic*, 13